EMANCIPATED

MY FAMILY'S FIGHT FOR FREEDOM

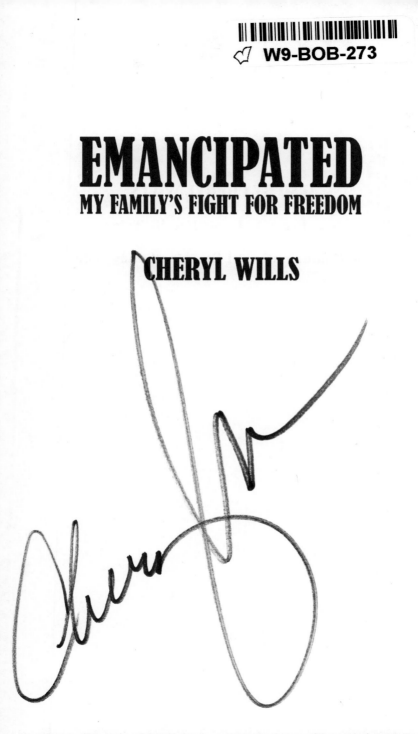

CHERYL WILLS

ALSO BY CHERYL WILLS

Die Free: A Heroic Family Tale

The Emancipation of Grandpa Sandy Wills

EMANCIPATED

MY FAMILY'S FIGHT FOR FREEDOM

CHERYL WILLS

Lightswitch
LEARNING
a Sussman Education company

150 East 52nd Street, Suite 32002
New York, NY 10022
www.lightswitchlearning.com

Educators and librarians, for a variety of teaching resources, visit www.lightswitchlearning.com.

Library of Congress Cataloging-in-Publication Data is available upon request. Library of Congress Catalog Card Number pending.

ISBN: 978-1-68265-354-8

Emancipated: My Family's Fight for Freedom by Cheryl Wills

Book design by Paula Jo Smith
The text of this book is set in Plantin Std.

Edited by Adam Reingold

Printed in Malaysia

2 3 4 5 6 7 8 9 10

To the soldiers who shaped me,

My Dad, SP4 Clarence Wills
(U.S. Army, 1962–1965)

My great-great-great Grandpa,
Private Sandy Wills
(United States Colored Troops, 1863–1866)

Grandpa Sandy's unheralded band of brothers:
Sgt. Dick Parker and James, Andy, Mack, and
Richard Wills

Great-great-great Grandma Emma,
a soldier in her own right (1851–1901)

And to the thousands of students whom I've met across the country, all those people who have embraced the story of my family's sojourn from slavery to freedom…

CONTENTS

WILLS FAMILY TREE

Direct Lineage: Sandy Wills to Cheryl Wills

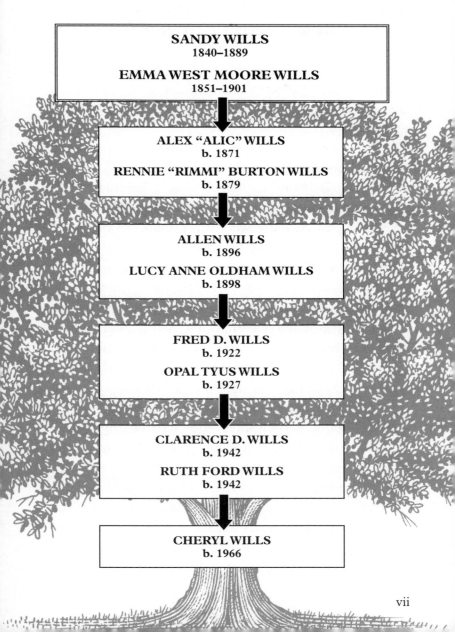

SANDY WILLS
1840–1889

EMMA WEST MOORE WILLS
1851–1901

↓

ALEX "ALIC" WILLS
b. 1871

RENNIE "RIMMI" BURTON WILLS
b. 1879

↓

ALLEN WILLS
b. 1896

LUCY ANNE OLDHAM WILLS
b. 1898

↓

FRED D. WILLS
b. 1922

OPAL TYUS WILLS
b. 1927

↓

CLARENCE D. WILLS
b. 1942

RUTH FORD WILLS
b. 1942

↓

CHERYL WILLS
b. 1966

FOREWORD

When I first met Cheryl Wills, she bounced through the doors at the African American Civil War Memorial and Museum in Washington, DC with a wonderful, wide-eyed enthusiasm. She then explained to me how she found her long lost great-great-great grandfather, Sandy Wills, who served as a member of the United States Colored Troops (USCT) from 1863 until the end of the war.

Cheryl's excitement touched my heart because I had devoted more than two decades to trying to establish this memorial from scratch. It was a herculean task that initially drew very little enthusiasm. But by the time we opened, there were more than ten thousand people at the celebration in 1998.

As I read Cheryl's latest book, *Emancipated: My Family's Fight for Freedom*, I was immediately impressed with her meticulous research and attention to detail. For example, Cheryl's Grandpa Sandy was one of many newly enlisted former slaves to take a bold step to declare themselves farmers, as opposed to slaves. I am deeply impressed that she decided to use such research as a teaching tool to inspire students!

Not many biographies are written by direct descendants of USCT soldiers, and that's one of the many reasons this book is a treasure! Indeed, Cheryl's passion for these warriors leaps off every page.

After President Abraham Lincoln signed the Emancipation Proclamation, more than two hundred thousand black men (formerly enslaved and freed blacks) took a leap of faith and volunteered to fight in President Lincoln's Union Army—which was on the ropes. The black troops brought new energy and much needed support and strength to the Northern army and ultimately helped save the Union.

That's why this book is so important generations later. Still so many people today don't know about the USCT. I wish I had read this book when I was a student because the author creatively weaves together two stories: the one about her Grandpa Sandy who fought in the Civil War and the saga of her paratrooper father who sadly went to his grave without knowing about his incredible family legacy.

At our museum, the centerpiece of our United States Colored Troops Memorial is a brilliant bronze statue depicting three black Union soldiers and one sailor. The statue is surrounded by a Wall of Honor, with stainless-steel plaques bearing the names of more than two hundred thousand black soldiers and their white officers who served in Lincoln's army. I'm proud to say that Cheryl's beloved great-great-great grandfather's name is there. When Private Sandy Wills was honorably discharged in 1866, the nation did not pause to salute Sandy or any of these heroes who helped to end slavery and keep America united under one flag. Seeing one of his descendants join us in giving thanks for his service is certainly heartwarming. This book is a testament to her enduring gratitude.

Dr. Frank Smith
Founder and Director
African American Civil War Memorial & Museum
Washington, DC
November 30, 2016

FREEDOM TIMELINE

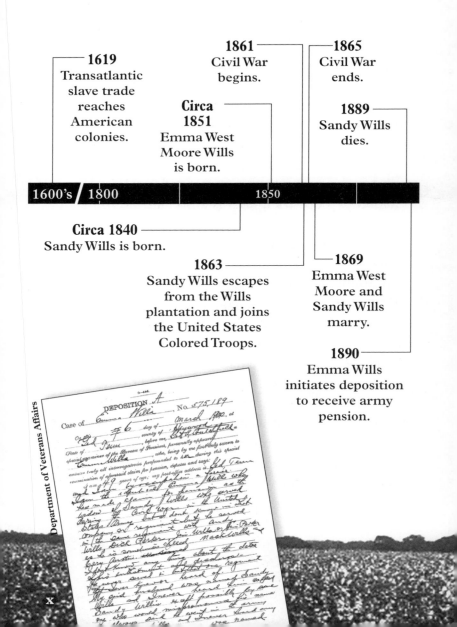

1619
Transatlantic slave trade reaches American colonies.

Circa 1840
Sandy Wills is born.

Circa 1851
Emma West Moore Wills is born.

1861
Civil War begins.

1863
Sandy Wills escapes from the Wills plantation and joins the United States Colored Troops.

1865
Civil War ends.

1869
Emma West Moore and Sandy Wills marry.

1889
Sandy Wills dies.

1890
Emma Wills initiates deposition to receive army pension.

1600's / 1800 | 1850

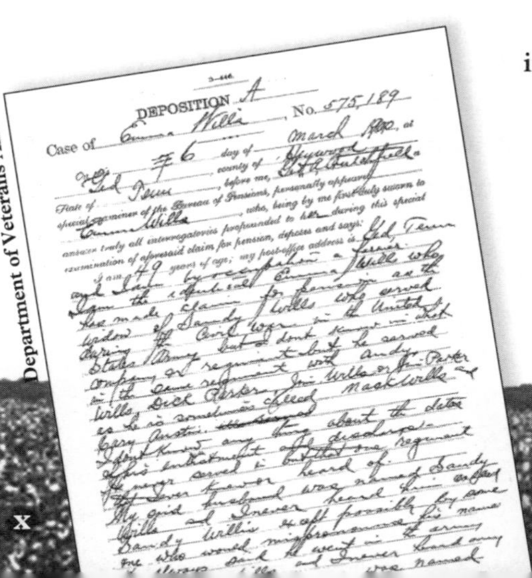
DEPOSITION A

Case of Emma Wills, No. 575,189

On this 6 day of March 1890, at ... county of Haywood, State of Tenn, before me, ... special examiner of the Bureau of Pensions, personally appeared Emma Wills, who, being by me first duly sworn to answer truly all interrogatories propounded to her during this special examination of aforesaid claim for pension, deposes and says: I am 49 years of age; my post-office address is ... Tenn

Department of Veterans Affairs

Wills Family Archives

1900 — 1950 — 2000

1901 Emma Wills dies.

1922 Fred Wills is born.

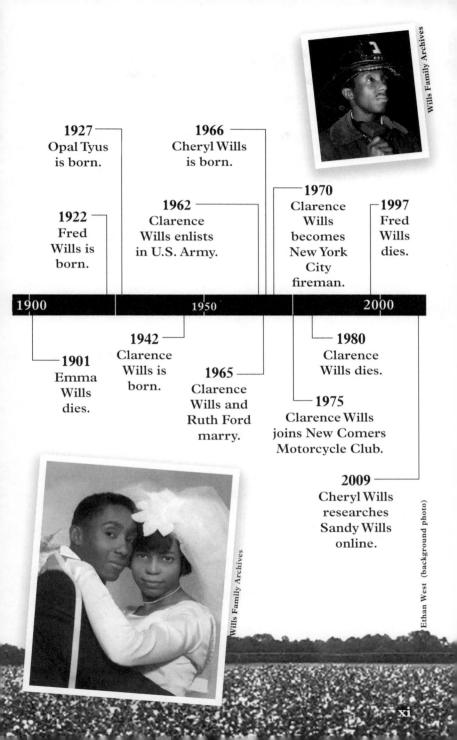

1927 Opal Tyus is born.

1942 Clarence Wills is born.

1962 Clarence Wills enlists in U.S. Army.

1965 Clarence Wills and Ruth Ford marry.

1966 Cheryl Wills is born.

1970 Clarence Wills becomes New York City fireman.

1975 Clarence Wills joins New Comers Motorcycle Club.

1980 Clarence Wills dies.

1997 Fred Wills dies.

2009 Cheryl Wills researches Sandy Wills online.

Wills Family Archives

Ethan West (background photo)

INTRODUCTION

As you will soon learn, I am obsessed with the legacy of my great-great-great grandparents, Sandy and Emma Wills. I wish I knew about their extraordinary heroism back when I was in school.

Grandpa Sandy and Grandma Emma had nine children. Nearly all of them had children of their own. Their second son, Alex, is the father of my grandfather's father, Allen. I am astounded when I think that Grandpa Sandy and Grandma Emma really didn't live that long ago and that many of our ancestors lived in the same area—Haywood County, Tennessee—for generations. My dad was born in Haywood County about fifty years after Grandpa Sandy died. Why didn't Alex tell Allen all about Grandpa Sandy and Grandma Emma? If he had done so, Allen most certainly would've told my Grandpa Fred, and I would have certainly found out about Grandpa Sandy's and Grandma Emma's heroism from my father.

This memoir is based on my own personal experiences as both a child and an adult. I also recreated, as best I could, the life of my ancestors based on research documents and primary sources I discovered. By telling my story in this way, I want students to be inspired to reconnect with the lost members of their own family trees. The experience is very liberating and empowering, believe me. I also encourage students to research and write essays, blogs, or even their own books about their families. Stop and think about it: No one wants to be forgotten—least of all by his or her own family. We all work hard and struggle to do better so that the next generation can soar even higher.

That struggle to do better is especially pronounced in African American families. Most of our family members in the past did not know how to read and write. They were even unable to sign their own names, much less document their family histories. For example, look at the back cover of this book. Do you see the first signature? It says, "Sandy Wills." But look closely in between his first and last names. It says, "his mark." All Grandpa Sandy was able to sign was the letter *X* for his signature. Regrettably, *X* was probably the only letter of the alphabet that Grandpa Sandy could identify.

I want people to know that Grandpa Sandy and Grandma Emma were not the only ones who signed their names with an *X*. Millions of Americans were denied the opportunity to attend school. I am honored in signing my name, which is also on the back of the book, as well as my dad's name.

Even though Grandpa Sandy and Grandma Emma were illiterate, they somehow made sure that their free children were able to read and write. This literacy is very special to me, and it's a very important milestone in my family.

I take tremendous pride in literacy. This book is my third. I love being an author and sharing my passion and my pain on paper. We can learn from our ancestors, even those who signed with an *X*.

Let's let the letter *X* stand for *eXcellent* in honor of all our ancestors.

Cheryl Wills

CHAPTER ONE

I Still Cry

Dear Mister Motorcycle Man,
You sped through life
Like a speeding train.
Why not stay with your wife
And come in from the rain?
I still cry.

When I was a little girl, one of my favorite uncles, my mother's brother, Aaron Ford, was murdered. He had five children—my cousins, of course—with whom I played every day. They lived in a building close to us in the same housing project. We sang lots of silly songs and played hand-clapping games together.

"I like coffee, I like tea, I like the colored boy, and he likes me."

But the smiles ended quickly. My cousins suddenly disappeared from my life. Mommy was too sad to talk about it. She had to walk by Uncle Aaron's building every day. She was so upset that she moved us to a nice new building not far away. Later, when I was old enough, I learned what really happened to my tall, freckled-faced uncle.

Like most of the kids I knew growing up, my cousins had a father no more. But I was lucky. I was proud to have a mother and father at home. Our new apartment was in a community called Ocean Village, which was in a neighborhood in New York City called Far Rockaway. It was like a gated paradise with white sand castles in the sky. We had a comfortable apartment on the second floor. From here, we breathed the sweet salt air and looked out on the deep blue water of the Atlantic Ocean across the street. Our community had a wading pool, a basketball court with four different baskets, a shopping center, and even a giant tree house with a seesaw. Although we had no real tree for our "tree house," city kids like us can imagine trees even when there are none. Our tree house had a soft, rubbery, pink floor. We played a game called "No Touching the Pink," which meant you had to run from the person trying to tag you, but you couldn't step on the pink floor of the tree house. If you did, you were "it." No one ever wanted to be "it."

My favorite game was "Hot Peas and Butter." Every kid I knew loved this game. All you needed was a leather belt and fast legs. As kids sat on the stoop or base, one person was selected to hide the belt in the parking lot. The belt was usually stashed away in a car bumper or under a loose hubcap. After hiding it, a kid returned to base and said, "Hot peas and butter, come and get your supper!" With that call, we all ran to find the belt. The person who hid it told us who's "hot," or near the belt, and who's "cold," or far away from it. Our game could go on for an hour or even more. Everyone was scared and excited. Best of all, the person who found the belt got to whip the other kids until they made it safely back to home base. In the summertime, if you were wearing shorts, you really felt the sting. I loved this game, and I loved our life. Not even the sting of a "hot peas" belt would stop me from smiling.

When we were older, we set garbage cans on fire on the beach and then watched the flames slowly fade into the dark, starry night. We had relay races on the rickety boardwalk, which was so close that it seemed to be part of our homes. We hit the beach for picnics and just to goof off every day, even on a school day. The boys played touch football in the sand, and the girls often walked along the jetties and watched the waves crash along the huge rocks. Sometimes, I would just sit alone on the boardwalk with my notebook in hand and stare out at the crashing waves, writing poems and wondering about all kinds of things.

We were happy kids. I had a happy family—for some time. We had such fun and felt very safe. We all looked out for one another. You knew your neighbors. It didn't matter that the streets were dingy and filled with cracks. I didn't even care that there were rats as big as cats in the neighborhood. We all knew our place. Our moms were quietly watching us no matter where we were. And when the streetlights came on and the sky turned dark throughout the neighborhood, you could hear our mothers loud and clear.

"Cheryl, come home."

"Gweek, Gweek, where are you?"

"Simone, it's enough, girl!"

At home, I was lucky to have the love of both parents. My mother loved my dad, Clarence Douglas Wills, so much that she had even given all of us names with his initials: I'm Cheryl Denise, the oldest kid in our family. Clarence Douglas Jr., named after my dad, comes next, but we call him Big Boy. Then there's Crystal Dianne and the twins, Celestial (Celeste) Daphne and Cleavon Daryl. Mom had trouble naming her last son, so she named him after a popular actor named Cleavon Little. And daddy, it seemed, was full of love, too.

I was always so proud of my mom and dad. Mommy always wore large, oversized, brown sunglasses. "Miss Fancy Pants" had style. Even though we lived in the projects, we had the most beautiful apartment, with custom-made drapes and fancy furniture. We also had expensive stereo equipment, like a reel-to-reel tape recorder and an 8-track tape player, to play our favorite music. Daddy liked gospel music and rhythm and blues, too, with singers like Marvin Gaye and Otis Redding. I loved the Jackson 5 and then Michael Jackson when he sang alone. Later, I liked some rappers too, especially Kurtis Blow.

Daddy was different from the other men in the neighborhood. Daddy's shoulders were always straight, and he walked straight, too. He didn't spend a lot of time hanging out and talking with others. Instead, he was always thinking about something, maybe of us, but also about other things I'll never really know. He was quiet and well-dressed...always.

Daddy was also very clean and neat. He was an army man, a brave paratrooper who jumped from airplanes and always landed on his feet. He had a system for everything. We all loved to watch him clean his teeth in the bathroom. We stared in silence, watching him in the mirror. With a machine called a Water Pik that squirted a jet of water from a small nozzle, daddy slowly sprayed between each tooth. Left side, right side. Top teeth, bottom teeth, then a rinse and a big white smile. All clean. Wow!

At the dinner table, daddy's place setting was arranged just as it was in the army: a glass of milk, a glass of water, and a clean and shiny knife, fork, and spoon. I wasn't quite sure why, but we each had a specific seat at the dining room table. Daddy sat at the head of the table by the window. I sat to his left. Crystal sat next to me; she's six years younger than I am. The twins, Celeste and Cleavon, sat in the two seats across from me. Mommy sat at the other head of the table, close to the kitchen. Big Boy never ate with us because he had difficulty sitting still. He always grabbed his hot dog or peanut butter sandwich and ate in his room or in the den. Daddy always had lots of questions for us. "Who's the president of the United States?" he'd ask. That question was an easy one. Then he'd ask, "Who are our senators?" That was a hard one!

I was also proud of my dad's profession. He was a fireman. I knew when he was about to come into the house because the scent of smoke arrived just before he did. The smell was special, mixed with the salt air of the Atlantic Ocean across the street.

Daddy's job made me nervous. I had bad thoughts in my head when I considered the work he did. When I was in kindergarten, we went to see daddy graduate from the fire academy. Mom was there. So was my brother, Big Boy, and my grandparents, Grandma Opal and Grandpa Fred Wills. Daddy was easy to spot. He and another man were the only black firefighters there. I watched him closely.

Daddy's graduation from the fire academy was very scary. I followed his every move. When he and the other firemen walked into a fake burning building, I screamed and cried. The audience was filled with Irish and Italian families, and lots of kids didn't seem to be scared of what they were seeing. I was terrified. I was all alone, as no one seemed to care about the men running into the burning building. With wide, adoring, tear-filled eyes, I thought my father with the handsome, dark face was going to die. I would continue to have this fear for a very long time.

By the time I was in third grade, we were a growing family. We were now five kids, and we all needed daddy's time and attention, including mommy. As his firstborn child, though, I felt he loved me most. When I took my first steps, I fell into his arms. He talked to me more than to the others. He always seemed more interested in me than in my brothers and sisters. Maybe it was because I was the oldest.

He always asked me questions like, "What do you want to be when you grow up?"

Of course, I then explained to him what I wanted to be. I had a habit of reading and cutting out newspaper articles from the New York *Daily News*. After I clipped them out, I would add my handwritten commentary at the bottom of the page of my loose-leaf notebook. I often read my words into a tape recorder. By recording my voice, I pretended to be a newscaster like Roger Grimsby or Bill Beutel on WABC's Channel 7 *Eyewitness News*.

"Oh, you mean you want to be a journalist?" he responded. I looked him in the eyes and said, "Oh, is that what being a newscaster is called?" I loved his questions. He just smiled at me, laughed, and told me that I would make a great reporter someday.

Daddy worked a lot. He was, of course, part of a group of men known as New York City's Bravest, a fireman. He was also in college as well as serving as a volunteer for the National Guard. In addition, daddy went to meetings with a group called the Masons. What he did there was secret. He would only say that he learned things at the meetings that made him a better person and that he didn't like to talk about it because, well, that was like bragging. Daddy didn't like bragging at all. He was also busy helping out at Grandma and Grandpa Wills' church along with his younger brother, Uncle Van.

On weekends, we left Far Rockaway and went to the church run by Grandma Opal and Grandpa Fred. The church was in Astoria, Queens, about thirty-five minutes from our apartment in Far Rockaway. Astoria was like another home for us. The church was on the street level, and their apartment was on the second floor, with lots of space and rooms.

Our grandparents' church was our playground. Grandma Opal and Grandpa Fred played games with us and always let us run up and down the church stairs. Grandma Opal had beautiful, deep-chocolate skin and a lovely, sparkling smile. She was sweet, kind, and strong as a rock, with a booming voice. And for someone with short, stubby fingers and fat hands, she sure tickled the ivories with amazing grace and power. Grandpa Fred was friendly and generous. With a slight limp, light-brown skin, high cheekbones, and a bony forehead, my Grandpa Fred reminded some kids of a scarecrow. But all the kids in the neighborhood smiled at Grandpa Fred, the man they called "Candy Man."

Along the side of the church, Candy Man built our favorite place in the world, his candy store. As he did with the church, Grandpa Fred built the store by hand with materials he found in the street and in junkyards, using a hammer, nails, and screwdrivers. He made it cozy for kids. The candy store wasn't fancy, but all that the kids really cared about anyway was the candy. Candy Man sold all kinds of candies and sodas, too. The store had a counter, with candy in jars behind a glass window. Kids from the neighborhood loved the store, and on Sundays, kids at church loved it, too. Grandpa Fred didn't even have a name for the store. Everyone just knew it was there. I loved Bazooka bubble gum and Blow Pops. Big Boy liked Snickers bars. Crystal loved the small caramels, and Cleavon liked Red Hots, Astro Pops, and even Violets, which tasted like flowers and would last a long time in your mouth. Celeste's favorites were the sweet butterscotch candies in the gold wrappers.

Most of all, I liked to stand next to Grandpa Fred as he sold the candies. I felt so important, like the store manager. We sold most candy for a nickel or dime. But some items, like Charleston Chews, were fifty cents. Grandpa Fred gave us the candies for free. Thanks, Grandpa!

On Saturdays, I would spend quiet time all alone with Grandma Opal, preparing for all the excitement of church on Sundays. I loved to weave her salt and pepper hair into a French braid, and I would smile as she often reminded me that she could have been a very famous singer. But she would always advise me that it was more important to stay home and take care of the family. She was happiest being home, not "singin' on the road."

Everyone seemed so proud of Grandpa Fred and Grandma Opal and of daddy and Uncle Van, too, for all the work they did to build the church. That the walls were tilted and crooked and painted a dull yellow didn't actually matter. No one really minded the naked lightbulbs hanging down or the exposed wiring wrapped in black electrical tape. We sat on wooden folding chairs, with cloth covers made by Grandma Opal fitted over the backs and hard, uncushioned pews that didn't match. The church wasn't fancy, but it was good enough. After all, everyone loved the music most of all. Awesome!

Sundays were the big day. Everyone dressed in his or her best. Daddy looked so good in a crisp suit and shiny shoes; he was always dressed perfectly. And so was mommy. She was so stylish in her outfits, unlike the other ladies dressed in long skirts and dresses covering their legs to the ankle. Makeup was discouraged, as was fancy jewelry. As a teenager, I was rebellious and wore lipstick, eyeliner, and even earrings. Shh! Boys wore pants and shiny shoes. No one wore sneakers.

At exactly 11:25 a.m., with the congregation seated, daddy would start to strum his guitar to be on key with Grandma Opal as she gently poked the piano keys. She'd hit a note, and daddy and Uncle Van would adjust their guitars. Grandma Opal was in charge, no doubt, but daddy was right behind her. He was focused and strong, like a military man on a mission. I could tell Grandma Opal and daddy were everyone's favorites at church.

And Grandpa Fred, Candy Man, was always ready to start the service—but just barely in time. All the kids were always begging him to open the candy store. And he couldn't say no to a kid. Yet no matter what, the service would begin. First, daddy would strum his guitar, and I would slowly lift my little tambourine, waiting for Grandma Opal to start. Then Grandpa Fred would appear suddenly, walking in quickly and grabbing his guitar.

Once she began singing, Grandma Opal always amazed everyone. Her alto voice was deep, strong, and clear as a bell. When she burst into song, she closed her eyes, opened her mouth wide, and really let it rip. I was so proud to sit next to her at the piano, swinging to the beat, accompanied by guitar back-ups from her dear boys: Grandpa Fred, daddy, and Uncle Van. Nearby, fast-talking Sister Sowell provided percussion as she beat on old pots and pans with a big spoon or stick.

Others quickly joined in and clapped their hands, while several boys played the bongos to keep time. When the music and the spirit in the church reached its climax, Grandma Opal would jump off the piano stool and dance to the gospel beat with her head bowed. I could only look on in amazement and happiness. Go Grandma!

When the music stopped, I was always very moved by the testimony service where, every week, people stood before the others to tell the most heartbreaking stories. They'd ask everyone to pray for them as they struggled in life. Some asked us to pray for a son or daughter who was struggling with drugs or alcohol. Others cried about a husband who disappeared or a job that was no more.

I admired these folks and their bravery. I began to understand their pain. After all, by fourth grade, I had a secret pain, a secret sadness at home, too. My daddy, Clarence, was changing. He and mommy argued a lot, and he was hardly ever at home. Eventually, he even left us and moved out. He was pretty slick about it, too. Clarence left most of his belongings at home and checked up on his five children every now and then.

In the sixth grade, when I was graduating from P.S. 225 Seaside Elementary School, Clarence didn't even bother to attend my graduation. I was so hurt and so disappointed—and scared and mad, too. Our hero Clarence, my daddy, seemed to love us no more.

Instead, he seemed to have a new family, a bunch of guys and some girls at his motorcycle club, the "New Comers." I felt like he loved them and his motorcycle more than his family. Even his love of gospel music seemed to fade away.

I was such a confused child and exposed to way too much tragedy for a thirteen-year-old girl. The only relief we felt was the sound of his motorcycle as he roared home to see us every once in a while. As he pulled up on the sidewalk near our apartment, all of the kids in Ocean Village stood back in amazement as my cool-looking dad, dressed in a leather jacket and bright red helmet, revved the engine to let everybody know he was home. With his leather boots and leather gloves, no one was cooler than our daddy, the easy rider, Clarence Douglas Wills.

And for a brief few minutes, I felt so excited, so safe, and so loved when he gave me a ride on his bike, slowly circling the parking lot. With my arms around his waist and a too-big helmet on my head, I was holding onto him real hard, hanging on, hoping he would stay forever. When other kids looked at his leather jacket and saw the name *New Comers* in big black letters on the back, they were impressed that "Mr. Motorcycle Man" was a member of a motorcycle club. For me, well, I was really angry. Clarence was spending more time with his motorcycle gang than with us. Not cool!

Once daddy moved out, mommy was all alone. She didn't smile much anymore and had a very short fuse. I was the biggest pain in the neck, because I was nosy and I asked a lot of questions. Only Grandma Opal offered me some comfort, telling me that Clarence was busy at work and that he still loved me. But I knew better. I knew the truth.

No one asked if I was hurting at the time, but I was almost as stressed out as my mother. I felt like a fatherless child, even though Clarence was still very much alive. I had been robbed of my childhood and was forced to deal with issues that I was not prepared to face. As much as I tried to have fun playing jump rope and "Hot Peas and Butter," I couldn't sleep at night. I just couldn't have fun.

At home, we needed Clarence more than ever. My sister Crystal started having seizures. At least once a week, I found her foaming at the mouth and shaking uncontrollably in her bed. She was barely four years old. We shared a room, and the sudden commotion always woke me up; I then made a mad dash down the hall to my mother's bedroom, crying for help. I was always in great pain seeing mommy weep with terror as she frantically lifted little Crystal out of her bed with her eyes rolled back and her Minnie Mouse pajamas twisted around her body. My job was to call 9-1-1 for help. Clarence was nowhere to be found.

Mommy spent hours alone in the emergency room with Crystal wrapped in a blanket, without any help from Clarence. Once, mommy had to make a decision about whether or not to let the doctors do a dangerous procedure, an operation called a spinal tap, to help Crystal. A spinal tap was risky to do on a little kid. Grandma Opal and Grandpa Fred, who did not believe in hospitalization or surgery of any kind, begged my mother not to let them operate on Crystal; however, mommy felt the surgery was necessary. My father Clarence did not even come by to visit Crystal in the hospital. She never forgot that it was only mommy at her bedside.

"You didn't come see me in the hospital, daddy!" Crystal cried when Clarence later handed her a present. Apparently, providing a gift was all he could do for us. On our birthdays and on Christmas, Clarence would show up with presents for all of us. Crystal never forgave Clarence, and neither did I.

My brother Big Boy was also in desperate need of his father. Big Boy's autism worsened with every birthday. Neighborhood kids who couldn't care less about his autism picked on him or beat him up. Mommy often ran outside in her robe and slippers to protect him. Helpless, we all stood in fear and watched mommy take on lots of bullies and troublemakers. Scared for mommy and feeling helpless, my little brother Cleavon would cry to himself at night, "I wish I was big. I wish I was big. I need a man to show me how to be strong." But no man showed up. Clarence was not home.

In time, Clarence tried to be a better dad. He moved some of his stuff back into the apartment and lived with us some of the time. But it was too late. One Sunday when I was thirteen years old, my mom decided to take us to our grandparents' church at the last minute. When I saw my daddy's motorcycle in front of the church, I ran up the stairs with my sisters and brothers behind me. Clarence was shocked to see us. He was with a woman we didn't know. Quickly, he tried to hide her in a side room in the apartment above the church. Mommy, though, saw her shadow. "Daddy, will you come downstairs and go to church with us?" I asked. Clarence didn't have a chance to respond as he looked at mommy's face. She yelled and cursed and put all of us back into the car. As she slammed the car door, she yelled, "I hope he drops dead!"

I cried the entire car ride back home. I hated my mother at that moment because I didn't understand why we had to leave. That confrontation was bad.

Even at church, no one dared to ask Grandma Opal about her older son, Clarence. "I guess Clarence is just like the rest of our kids," they quietly whispered to each other.

Our loving and fun dad was disappearing. The dutiful son and church deacon was now in a motorcycle gang. The great guitarist, who played the most beautiful melodies that some folks had ever heard, now hid his instrument in the back of the closet. Our brave army paratrooper, who jumped from airplanes, was falling out of control with no parachute.

The situation kept getting worse. One summer day, Clarence was supposed to come home by noon to give me money so I could buy a new outfit for the first day of school. I was so excited for my last year at Junior High School 180 in Rockaway Beach. Mommy was going to drive me to the mall. Her mother, Grandma Sallie, was all ready to babysit while we were out. Everything was all set. But where was Clarence? I sat by the window, waiting for the rumble of his motorcycle. He had totally promised me that he would be there by noon. I sat and waited. By three o'clock, Clarence hadn't arrived. By four o'clock, he was nowhere to be found. Two hours later at six o'clock, Mr. Motorcycle Man still hadn't arrived. Soon it was seven o'clock, and the stores were closing.

Then the phone rang. My mother picked it up. Mommy was elegant, but she was also from the Bronx. Whoa! She really cussed at Clarence. "Don't you know she's been sitting in the window waiting for you all day," she yelled at him. "Now you tell her!" she warned Clarence. I picked up the phone and heard his voice.

"Hi Cheryl, listen, I'm sorry. I'll be there tomorrow. I had to work. I'm coming tomorrow. Okay?"

I had only one response: "Okay."

I slammed down the phone receiver and screamed, "I hope he drops dead!"

I didn't really mean what I had said, but enough was enough. This man had hurt me and all of us too much, for too long. He missed our date, and he also missed Big Boy's birthday, which was the day before, on the third of September. His letting us down was a new low. That he had moved all of his stuff back home didn't really matter. He still didn't keep his word. We were just little kids, but we were hurting.

Grandma Sallie looked at me in disgust. Her face said it all. She thought my mother had spoiled us rotten. I didn't care what she or anyone else thought. I was sick of not knowing where my daddy was half the time. I went into my room and slammed the door shut. Then I smacked the last gift he gave me, a beautiful black doll with a ruby-red, Victorian-style gown.

Words didn't mean anything, right? I did not have magical powers, right? What's the big deal? Once, a girl bullied me and made me cry; I told my friends the same thing I said when Clarence missed our date, and she was still alive. So no big deal, right? I mean, who thinks someone's gonna drop dead when you wish such a thing?

CHAPTER TWO

Why?

Dear Father,
You were a combustible soul
And a part-time pop.
In our hearts you left a hole.
When will your madness stop?
I can only ask, "Why?"

Of course, who would want anyone dead? I didn't really wish daddy dead, but I was mad and hurt. I had waited all that hot, late summer day, sitting by the window, waiting for the roar of his motorcycle. Silence. He never showed up. That day was a long, mean one. As I tried to fall asleep that night, I looked forward to the next day. It couldn't be any worse.

Later that night at around midnight, the phone rang at our apartment. *Who would be calling a woman with five children at such a late hour?* I thought to myself. As daddy always reminded me, I was nosy all right. So when mommy picked up the phone in her room, I ran to another phone and secretly listened in on the call. I quickly heard a man named Deacon Edward Brown on the other end of the phone say to mommy, "I'm so sorry, Ruth."

"Sorry for what?" mommy replied.

He was startled by her response and hung up suddenly. Mommy then quickly called and woke up her mother, Grandma Sallie, and warned her that something bad had happened.

I was so anxious and confused. Events were all happening so fast. I had no idea how to express my concern. Adults are supposed to be in charge, not kids. However, I had always worried about my father, almost like I was his parent. Now my worst fears had been confirmed.

Mommy then tried to call Grandma Opal and Grandpa Fred but got no answer. My heart started racing. In my mind, I was trying to reassure myself that "this is not happening." Then about forty minutes later, the phone rang again. It was Grandpa Fred.

"Ruth, Clarence got into some kind of accident," he said abruptly, not telling us the truth and secretly hoping that the news was all a big mistake.

Grandpa Fred then said he'd find out more and call back. When the phone rang again about twenty minutes later, I picked it up almost before mommy did. "The boy is dead," Grandpa Fred simply said.

Whoa! I felt a shock go up my spine into my brain. I couldn't believe what I had just heard. Then mommy responded in her soft, gentle voice, "Oh, no!"

The message was so final, so horribly final. No backsies for me.

I hung up the phone, the very same phone I had wished my father dead on, the very same phone my father had lied to me on for the last time just a few hours earlier. I ran to my bedroom and cried my heart out. His death was so final, so quick. Hearing my painful wailing, mommy entered the bedroom, realizing she didn't even have to tell me about daddy.

Soon, my sisters and brothers woke up, except for Big Boy. He heard me cry, but he just rolled over and continued to sleep. When mommy explained to Crystal, Cleavon, and Celeste that our daddy was dead, they collapsed on my bed and cried, too. Mommy then tried to calm us down by rubbing our backs and telling us that everything would be okay even as the phone began to ring off the hook.

On Thursday, September 4, 1980, Clarence Douglas Wills died the day after his son Clarence Jr.'s twelfth birthday, the same day he lied to me about having to be at work and not being able to see me. Daddy was dead. I would never wish anyone dead again.

Daddy had sealed his fate years ago when he decided that he preferred to be in the company of those he called his "other" family, a bunch of guys at the New Comers Motorcycle Club. This other family had the privilege of being the last to see daddy alive. Just before midnight on that warm summer night, daddy's strong body flew off his motorcycle after a collision with a car on the Williamsburg Bridge in New York City. The strap of his fancy half-helmet (he was too cool to wear a full helmet) had become loose, turning into a noose around his neck, almost tearing his head off. Daddy drew his last breath on that old, ugly bridge 125 feet above the city. Daddy was handsome no more.

On the following days, we were all numb. We missed the first day of school. Labor Day weekend was no fun because we were all so sad. All kinds of folks kept coming by to visit us at home, including lots of white people. So much food was in the kitchen, and so many people were jammed into the dining room and living room. Strangers were washing our dishes and even using our bathrooms.

Seven days later, on Thursday, September 11, 1980, I sat in complete shock in the front pew of the Refuge Church of Christ on Mott Avenue in Far Rockaway for daddy's funeral. I wore a white blouse and a black pleated skirt. My Uncle David's girlfriend pressed my hair, a job that my mother usually did. This woman was so nice to tell me that my hair had such great body. Her compliment was the first that I had ever received about my hair.

The funeral was such a spectacle that I didn't have a moment to cry. The police shut down the roads leading to the church for hours. Police cars, fire department vehicles, army trucks, limousines, daddy's black hearse, and hundreds of motorcycles of all colors with shiny metal and fancy paint jobs were all lined up in front of the church. The thunder of the motorcycle engines sounded like miniexplosions causing the mourners to turn their heads. Unbelievable!

The funeral was led by Elder Leroy Joseph, a man whom daddy had deeply respected. Elder Joseph had tried to talk sense into daddy as he struggled to find his way in the world.

We must have looked like vulnerable and scared little ducklings as we walked in line to the front pew following mommy. She sat to our left. As always, she looked stunning with her big, brown sunglasses and an elegant outfit. Her youngest brother, Uncle David, sat to her left. Throughout the funeral, mommy stared straight ahead. She was more angry than sad.

My four younger sisters and brothers were seated to my right. We were a most heart-wrenching sight, each of us dressed in our Sunday finest, with our legs dangling from the church bench. We had no idea how powerful this single moment would be for each of us in the days and decades to come. Right behind us, in the second pew, sat Grandma Opal, Grandpa Fred, and Uncle Van. Also behind us were mommy's parents, Grandma Sallie and Grandpa Hardy. Grandma Sallie was a light brown, statuesque woman with a high-pitched voice and beautiful eyes. Her cheeks were always naturally rosy, and so were her lips. She dressed as elegantly as she could while remaining obedient to the religious code. Grandpa Hardy was tall, with very dark-colored skin, and he walked with perfect posture. He was stern, and Grandma Sallie was gentle.

Daddy was about ten feet away from us, lying in a shiny blue-gray casket. I wouldn't wish that day on anybody. I had no idea how badly mangled daddy was until three funeral directors carefully positioned their bodies in front of his casket before they opened it. I sneaked a look and watched their every move as they gently opened it with all six hands. Then they did something to daddy's head. It looked like they were putting his head back on his neck and adjusting the shiny steel pins to keep it in place. And then they stepped away. I got a full view from my seat. I almost fainted.

I wasn't sure if that man in the dark blue suit really was my beautiful, mocha-colored daddy. His hair started way at the top of his head, with stitches everywhere. Daddy's soft, almond eyes were sewn shut, his nose was crooked, and his skin color was blacker than he really was. Oh my!

Why do they have to show my daddy to everyone? I wondered. I kept inching up from my seat to get a good look. I still wasn't sure that daddy was really daddy. I guess I had become a distraction because Grandpa Fred tapped me on the shoulder and shook his head, signaling for me to stop.

Carefully, I assessed everyone who walked passed us to visit with daddy for the last time. Then the mourners came forward to pay their respects to mommy, whispering a few kind words and sometimes handing her an envelope with money. Each one of them looked at the five of us children with terrible sadness. We were alone and numb, and they knew it. People we didn't even know just couldn't believe what they were seeing and feeling. One black man stood in the long line three times to see my father in his casket. *How did he know daddy?* I wondered. Each time he looked down at the casket, he shook his head in disbelief. Then he walked around the church and stood in the line again. Yes, Clarence was gone.

I didn't know what else to expect at the funeral, but I sure was hoping that there would be no outbursts, shrieks, or loud crying. Mommy shed one tear, nothing more. I know because I watched her tear slowly trickle down her cheek. I guess everyone expected Grandma Opal to break down at the sight of her dead son, but she did not. Daddy was her oldest son, but she had buried two of her other children years earlier.

She was tough. And I bet many thought that we kids would cry or scream, too. Not us. Nothing. We were too confused, too scared. Even our tears were locked away in confusion. Only one person in the family wept—Grandpa Fred. At first, I heard him sniffling in the pew behind me. When I slowly turned around, I was shocked to see him with his head in his hands. Grandpa had never before lost control of his emotions. I had never even seen him cry or even come anywhere close to being emotional. Grandma Opal rubbed his back as he quietly drowned in his tears. Poor Grandpa!

Looking around inside the large church, I couldn't quite understand from where all the people had come. It was packed with nearly one thousand mourners, squeezed shoulder to shoulder in the pews and standing in rows all along the aisles. The church was really crowded and was also such a fire hazard. But who would complain? All of the "City's Bravest," the New York City Fire Department, were right there with daddy in the church. As a respected firefighter, daddy was given a funeral complete with an escort of twelve members of the fire department and one fire lieutenant, all so formal and handsome. Hundreds of other firefighters were there, too, in their perfect, dark blue uniforms and dark blue caps to say goodbye to daddy.

Red-eyed Irish and Italian men cried for daddy, the man they initially had hated when he bounded through the doors of Engine 1, Ladder 24, on West 31st Street, just around the corner from Madison Square Garden. He was among the first wave of black firefighters to join that firehouse in New York City. In his first couple of years in the firehouse, the previously all-white unit gave the "colored guy," as they called him, a lot of grief.

Long after daddy proved their prejudices wrong through his hard work and quiet dignity, his fellow firefighters briefly glanced at us as they gently carried their fallen hero to the front of the church. I didn't know what to think. I just stared at them. Whoa! So many men in uniforms attended the funeral. I saw not only firefighters, but also neatly dressed men from the U.S. Army with all kinds of fancy pins and medals on their green uniforms. They, too, were here to pay their respects to their hero, a staff sergeant who earned his two stripes and paratrooper wings through hard work, sacrifice, and fearlessness. Daddy had enlisted in the army on a whim to spite Grandpa Fred, who had ticked him off one too many times. Enlisting was the only way to get out from under his father's roof and to move forward with his ambitions without making a mess of his life.

Dozens of ugly men in black leather vests from daddy's motorcycle club were also standing along the aisles. I was so angry to see them. They disgraced the church by not even wearing suits. These disrespectful, long-haired, wild things looked especially frightening to us as they stood quietly with black fabric on the back of their vests covering the name of their motorcycle club, "New Comers." I eyeballed them with disgust. The way I saw it, they had killed my daddy. Now they were desecrating the church with their filthy and intimidating appearance. "Get Out! Get Out!" I wanted to yell and scream at them, but I knew my grandparents would not have approved of my rudeness.

Further behind us was a sea of brown and black downcast faces, people who loved daddy throughout his short life. There were poor, old church ladies, some dressed in black and others in white in the tradition of their African ancestors, women who had delightfully danced and sung along with daddy's guitar at church. Young men whom daddy had trained to sing in gospel quartets, as well as young ladies whom he taught at Sunday school, also attended the funeral. I noticed, too, many neighbors from Far Rockaway.

During the service, I was happy to see many of the amazing vocalists and musicians from Grandpa Fred's church. Seeing them was comforting. I very well understood why they were speechless and too sad to sing or play their instruments. Somehow though, probably out of respect and love for Grandma Opal, the church's adult choir was able to find the strength to sing one of daddy's favorite church songs. Without Grandma Opal's beautiful voice, they sounded terrible. Still, the nine church ladies and two men in the choir tried their best as they mourned more for Grandma Opal, whom they loved like a mother, rather than for her misguided son.

Typically, church singing inspires people to rise to their feet and sing. But on this sorrowful day, no one had the strength to stand, let alone sing. Then Elder Joseph's lovely, soft-spoken wife Judy stood up to read a dull obituary—an unintentional slap in the face to my father's amazing legacy. I was so mad. Her intentions were good, but daddy deserved much more.

Judy began:

Clarence Douglas Wills was born April 18, 1942, to Fred and Opal Wills in Brownsville, Tennessee. He was educated in the Cleveland, Ohio, school system and Bryant High School, New York. He was a graduate of the following colleges: International Data Processing Institute; New York City Community College; and John Jay College of Criminal Justice. He was also a 32-degree Mason of Mt. Lebanon Lodge No. 173 of New York City. Clarence's work record was as manager of the United Parcel Service in New York and a member of the Greater New York City Fire Department and of the National Guard of the United States. At the time of his death, he was on active duty in all of the above. His church memberships were as follows: Refuge Church of Christ, Arverne, New York, Elder Leroy Joseph, pastor; Light House Church of Christ, Elder Fred D. Wills, pastor; and the Life Science Church, Lynbrook, Long Island, New York. Clarence was a loving husband, a devoted father, and a dedicated son and brother. He was a dedicated worker, kind and generous, and a friend to all who knew him. To know him was to love him. Besides his family, Clarence's loves were his job, fighting fires, and riding his motorcycle. Clarence departed this life on Thursday, September 4, 1980, leaving to mourn: a wife, Ruth Naomi, and five children: Cheryl Denise, thirteen; Clarence Douglas, twelve; Crystal Dianne,

> eight; Cleavon Daryl and Celestial Daphne, six-year-old twins; his mother and father, Opal Virginia Tyus Wills and Fred Douglas Wills; one brother, Van Luster Wills; eight aunts; eleven uncles; mother-in-law and father-in-law Elder and Sister Hardy Ford; nieces, nephews, sisters-in-law, brothers-in-law, and a host of other relatives and friends.

What a crock! Sorry, Sister Judy! This astonishingly brief outline of my father's life was not enough! My spirited daddy lived a crazy, fast-paced life. He had jumped feet first out of airplanes miles high. He had mastered the ancient rituals and rites of the Freemason's organization. My father contributed an unforgettable thread to the African American experience by reaching great heights. Of course, he reached new lows, too, but even though I was angry with him, he deserved a better goodbye. The obituary, which was formatted on a single eight-by-eleven sheet of paper, was folded in half with a picture of a Bible on front. One of daddy's beautiful photos wasn't even printed on the front cover! He left behind thousands of amazing pictures of every year of his life. Clearly, only we really knew daddy.

Thankfully, the funeral finally came to an end. At last, we could be alone with daddy.

Uncle Van and Grandpa Fred calmly walked with Grandma Opal to get one last look at the son and brother who had become the leader of the family. They said a final goodbye to the child who had come closest to fulfilling the family's dream.

Grandma Opal tenderly stared at the third of her four children to be snatched from her tight grip. She whispered something to daddy, but he was silent, unable to respond to the mother he loved so dearly, the person he trusted more than anyone else.

When Grandma Opal and Grandpa Fred slowly walked away, the funeral directors motioned for mommy and us to step forward and visit daddy. As the oldest, I made a quick judgment call. In one swift motion with my head, I looked at my sisters and brothers and softly said, "We're not going up there."

We sat quietly as mommy and her brother David walked slowly up to daddy to say a final goodbye. I knew that the horrible sight of our father's body would be stuck in our hearts and minds forever. The view from ten feet back was bad enough. All of my siblings obeyed me, except sweet Crystal. She was eight years old and felt bad that mommy stood there without her children. As Crystal bolted from her seat towards the casket, I warned her, "You'll be sorry."

When would this horror show end? I was two weeks shy of my fourteenth birthday. I had missed the first week of school, and now I had to live the rest of my life as a fatherless child. *What had I done to deserve my daddy's death at such a young age?* I asked myself. Finally back at school, all of my friends asked me where I had been. "My father died," I calmly replied to all who asked. Their response was always the same—"Ooh!"

Soon after the funeral, I went to my grandparents' house to see what daddy had left behind in his last days and hours. Although he had moved most of his belongings back to our apartment in Far Rockaway, I was able to touch the last things he had touched: his notebooks, textbooks, and pens of different colors. A half-cup of old coffee was on his bedside table next to his cufflinks and unwashed blue fireman shirts. I wondered if he knew I was there visiting, wanting to just say hi and be close to him again. When I left daddy that day, I was sad and scared. I would feel that way for a very long time.

Following daddy's death, our family had more upheavals. Shortly after he died, some thugs broke into our apartment in Far Rockaway and stole everything they could, including mommy's wedding ring and almost all of daddy's fancy stereo equipment. They even took a two-dollar bill that Uncle David had given me for good luck that I had taped to my bedroom wall. I guess that two-dollar bill wasn't really so lucky!

Mommy had had enough. Soon she moved us to a house in Hempstead, Long Island, a suburb of New York City. A few months later, Grandma Opal and Grandpa Fred also moved out of their big house and church that I had loved to a new much smaller place on Astoria Boulevard in Queens, New York. With images of daddy's mangled body still fresh in my mind, all these changes were too much.

I hated our new neighborhood in Hempstead at first. But I quickly made friends with great girls like Gabriella Phelps, Debra Porter, and Kim West. I was surprised a few months later to also hear that some of my old friends from Far Rockaway, like Eddie Torres and Kelda Savage, had moved to the suburbs as well.

Mommy tried to go on with her life and to date men but to no avail. I gave each of them a very difficult time, and my siblings also helped run each and every one of them away. My duty was to protect daddy's turf and memory, and no man was going to take his place. All of us were rude, refusing to talk with her suitors. Mommy tried to control us, but she was outnumbered. She knew we were all too grief-stricken to be ignored.

We were lucky, though, that Grandpa Fred became a perfect grandfather and surrogate father to us all. He made my teenage years survivable. He bought a new van and took us everywhere—to church conventions in other states, to relatives in Ohio, and up and down the East Coast, including Disney World in Orlando, Florida. He again built a new storefront church with his own hands and shared it all with us. Every Sunday, he arrived in Hempstead to take us to church and then returned us back home again. In time, Uncle Van joined us at church and played his guitar alongside his father and mother. It was bittersweet, though, because daddy's absence was strong. The beautiful church music just didn't sound the same without his guitar-playing.

Grandpa Fred saw how terribly daddy's death impacted us, so he made sure to never let us down. After church, he bought us pizza and hamburgers. Grandpa Fred also gave each of us an allowance of a few dollars. If he promised something, he did it, and we became almost happy kids again.

We had lost a father, but we gained an amazing grandfather in return. When I later graduated from junior college, Grandpa Fred made sure that he sat in an empty section where I could see him. Then he could wave at me, and I could wave back, which we did to each other about a dozen times. Thank you, Grandpa Fred!

Later, when I went off to Syracuse University to study journalism, Grandpa Fred was right there with me, too. Every summer, he would pack his church van to the roof and haul all of my stuff to my college dorm almost three hundred miles away in upstate New York and then come back again every May to take me home. At my graduation inside Syracuse University's Carrier Dome in 1989, he was as proud as any man could be. Many thought he was my father, and, in many ways, he was. Daddy's spirit was enveloped inside him, body and soul. Our Grandpa Fred took care of his grandchildren in a way that would have made his son very proud. I could not have asked for a better grandfather.

Yes, we were happier. But I always knew and I always felt that those whom we loved the most could disappear or be taken away at any time. The past years had taught my siblings and me to build walls, all to protect ourselves from being hurt.

In 1997, Grandpa Fred had a cough that wouldn't quit, but he refused to see a doctor. He was stubborn for sure. Within a few months, for the first time ever, he didn't even have the strength to go downstairs to church and preach on Sunday mornings. He had become just skin and bones.

"I can't keep any food down—everything I put in my mouth tastes like cotton," he said to me. I was frustrated with him and begged him to see a doctor. He again refused. Scared and sad, I finally told him,

"Well, if you can't eat, you will surely die. So if you still don't understand why you should see a doctor now, then Grandma will find you dead in the bed!"

Finally, he allowed us to take him to Astoria General Hospital where an X-ray revealed he had lung cancer. The tumor had spread from his lungs to his throat and was literally choking him to death. Worse still, it was inoperable. The doctors wanted to admit him for treatment, but he refused. When we returned from the hospital, I helped him back to his bed, where I saw dozens of cough drops on his nightstand. Poor Grandpa Fred had been using the throat lozenges to relieve his deadly cancer symptoms. During my visits with him, we spoke about life and many other things. Once he sadly told me, "I guess we weren't meant to have nuth'in." His remark stunned me because I didn't know that he actually wanted anything more than what he had. I was sad to hear that Grandpa Fred felt his life had been a failure.

Over his nearly seventy-five years, Grandpa Fred had gained little but lost much—the worst loss being his firstborn son, my daddy. Grandpa Fred really wanted to be a big-time preacher with a large church, but he never succeeded. I tried to bring as much sunshine into his life as I could. After all, he was so good to us.

Even after the tragedy of my father's death, Grandpa Fred managed to have some good times together with us. But in his final analysis, I suppose it wasn't what he had expected. His sad words revealed to me that he died a disappointed and unfulfilled man. I was very sorry that I didn't have the power to change

Grandpa Fred's attitude because he really deserved more. Maybe he beat himself up over daddy's death and never got over it.

Up until the day he died on March 17, 1997, Grandpa Fred constantly struggled to be a better man—the best way he knew how. He tried to educate and better himself by reading dictionaries and encyclopedias. Sometimes, he failed miserably, but he never stopped reaching. In my view, Grandpa Fred succeeded most of the time, more than any man I knew of in the Wills family.

Grandma Opal and Grandpa Fred were so kind to us and helped us to survive. Yet my teenage years felt very unnatural. We had to survive without daddy. Teenagers are not adults, but I had to act like an adult. In one way, I felt strong and proud to be counted on to help mommy raise our family. However, the responsibility also made me feel different from others I knew. Feeling different was uncomfortable.

Deep inside, I was still the little girl crying into her tambourine, listening carefully for the sweet beat of her father's music. I was very close to him, and I was also very proud of him. Underneath my anger and sadness, it felt good to know that daddy did things in his life that were wonderful—or most of the time I think so, anyway.

Our hearts remained broken for a very long time. We couldn't even imagine that one day, another man in the Wills family would step into our lives and make us smile once again.

CHAPTER THREE

Same Bloodline, Different Times

Clarence and Sandy:
One was born into slavery and died free,
by his own might.
The other was born free and died enslaved,
by his own mind.
Same bloodline, different times.
Fighting two wars,
On two different shores.

My fathers—a century apart—battled two uncivil wars with one clear victory and one terribly humiliating defeat.

When daddy left me for good on that awful September day in 1980, I was numb, confused, and in pain. We all were. The men in our family seemed doomed. These were not good times to be a Wills man. Daddy disappeared like a thief in the night. In the end, Grandpa Fred felt he had achieved "nuth'in" in life. We didn't know much about our Uncle Van, as he was shy and quiet, a silent witness to perhaps too much in life. However, he did love daddy and understood him better than anyone else did. We did know, though, that like the other Wills men in our family, Uncle Van wasn't quite sure how to show his emotions. Hurt as he was, he didn't shed a single tear at daddy's funeral.

As for the other Wills men, my brothers Big Boy and Cleavon, well, they really needed the attention and strength of an older man. Cleavon never forgot how much mommy and all of us suffered without daddy around. Cleavon admired the way mommy stood up to all the bullies who picked on Big Boy in Far Rockaway. He cried and worried plenty that he wasn't big enough to protect us.

In truth, though, we had no expectations and no understanding really about what it meant to have a father to help guide us. As we got older, we each in our own way searched for bridges to connect our past to our present lives. None of us dared to imagine that another man with the last name of Wills could possibly change our lives once again.

Yet let me be clear: My childhood wasn't all bad. My father started out as a model dad before he lost his way. He was awesome until I was about eight years old. I received most of his attention, as my other siblings were not born until a few years after me. My brothers and sisters never had the benefit of his guidance, as I did. I was the first girl in the family in a generation, for Grandma Opal only had two boys. My dad understood men better than he understood women, so I was an anomaly to him. Yet he was totally enthusiastic about me and expressed big plans for me. He wanted me to go to college and to be rich. Most of the family was dirt poor, and my father hated poverty. He also had excellent diction, and he taught me to speak properly. He hated slang and slow talkers. I remember how he taught me all kinds of things like vowels and parts of speech. However, daddy didn't really know how to cope with the challenges of Big Boy's autism. By the time my sister Crystal was born in 1972, daddy was riding his motorcycle and popping wheelies far away from home.

When I became a television reporter in New York City in the 1990s, I used my maiden name Wills as a tribute to my dad. My husband John was slightly offended, but I made it clear to him that my loyalty to my father's legacy was extremely important to me. The name Wills was all I had left from daddy. It was, in some ways, all that any of us had left. He knew a million people during his short lifetime. I hoped someone might recognize the name and wonder if that "news lady"—as I'm often called in the street—was Clarence Wills's daughter.

As a TV journalist, I slowly mastered the art of telling stories about people and finding out what makes them tick. I reported many stories about people who did notorious things and others who went above and beyond their responsibilities to help others. All along, I could feel daddy's spirit pushing me to tell his special story. I had started and stopped writing his biography so many times. The last one I attempted was titled *The Sins of the Firefighter*, but I never finished it. Something was holding me back. I was scared and looking for direction, trying to understand the past in order to save my future. Often, I heard my father, ever the paratrooper, telling me not to be scared: "Jump, daughter, and figure out how to land later!"

In 2006, I reported a story on a company called African Ancestry that enabled people to trace their family roots using DNA analysis. As part of my interview with the company, I had the inside of my cheek swiped with a cotton swab. Then the swab was submitted into the company's DNA database. Based on the results, I was given a certificate that claimed that I was a partial paternal descendant of the Bamileke people in the area that today is the African nation of Cameroon. I thought this discovery was very interesting, but it really didn't give me a crystal clear picture of exactly who I was. During the transatlantic slave trade beginning about four hundred years ago, Africans from all over the west coast of Africa and beyond were all mixed together—human trafficking was not separated by ethnicity, tribe, or religion. So through the ensuing years in many countries that adopted slavery, including our own, Nigerians mixed with people from Cameroon, and folks from Senegal mixed with people from Ghana—and so on. While one thin thread of my DNA indicated a Cameroonian link, many other holes in my ancestry remained unknown. But one thing was clear: I had a need never to forget my father and to know more about my ancestors.

Twenty-five years had passed since my father's death, and I was finally happier. My eyes were opening up to the world. I was less scared. I was like a paratrooper, "jumping" a bit more, although I wasn't quite landing. Still, I felt honored to call myself a daughter of Africa. Unlike my parents or grandparents, I was becoming outwardly proud of my heritage. I had no need to hide my origins. When Grandma Opal danced in church, she had little interest in knowing that her fancy footsteps were set in motion long ago in Africa. The swivel of her hips and the songs that bounced off her tongue were not indigenous to North America. Instead, they were likely linked to a colorful and vibrant African tribe that none of us could identify. Grandma Opal's round, stunning face and deep chocolate color came from a continent that she dared not mention. Her music, her laughter, her strength—it was all from Mother Africa. And these attributes were something of which to be proud, not ashamed.

One afternoon several weeks before my son John's twelfth birthday in 2009, I was casually surfing online when I landed on a website that caught my attention: "ancestry.com." I really wasn't on a particular mission. I was just killing time at home during an otherwise gray November day. I signed in to the website and started to poke around.

Unsure of what to do, I clicked on a simple header labeled, "Search." It enabled me to find ancestors from the past. Cool. I was intrigued.

Then a drop-down window appeared with several options such as:

"All Collections."

"Census and Voter Lists."

I clicked on "All Collections."

Nice.

Then another drop-down window appeared, asking for "first name," "last name," "city or county," and "birthdate."

Not sure of what to do, I first typed in my last name, "Wills."

Then I typed in "Haywood County, Tennessee," knowing that my father's family came from there.

I ignored the birthdate box because I knew very little about my family's past in Haywood County.

Next, I clicked on a big gold button labeled, "Search." Hmmm, interesting.

Many names were listed under the document category "United States Federal Census 1840."

I guessed that I needed names listed in a more recent census. So I scrolled to find "United States Federal Census 1880." I clicked on it. Whoa!

I scrolled through the names listed: "Mary Wills," "Thomas Mills," and "William D. Wills."

Now what? So I scrolled down some more. More names appeared: "James Wills," "Andy Wills," "Mack Wills," "Dick Wills," and "Richard Wills."

Then I saw another name that really caught my attention: "Sandy Wills."

"Who is that?" I wondered. The name Sandy stuck out because it was an odd name for a black man in the nineteenth century. Most newborn boys were given biblical names like John, Matthew, or Thomas. I had no idea if I was related to any of these people. Maybe it was just a coincidence that they all were from Haywood County, Tennessee, just like my father and Grandpa Fred.

Next, I searched for the same names under the section for military records. Wow, I again found their exact names, and all were identified as being involved with the United States Colored Troops (USCT)! In 1863 during the Civil War, soldiers in the USCT were part of the U.S. Army, made up of African American soldiers who previously were slaves. Could I possibly be related to former slaves who actually fought against slavery during the Civil War?

Being a reporter, I was very intrigued. Yet as a weary member of the Wills family, I instantly feared getting my hopes up about Sandy Wills. Such a link seemed too good to be true. I wasn't the lucky type. The odds of being related to a historical figure like Sandy Wills felt about the same as someone telling me that Michael Jackson was my uncle.

I needed to know more. But before telling anyone about my findings, I worked with a genealogist named Craig Rice to determine if perhaps I had a real connection to Sandy Wills. Craig warned me that he might take a long time to complete his research. I was fine with his warning. I was more worried that he just wouldn't be able to find out anything more about Sandy Wills. Daddy, "I'm jumping!"

The next day, Craig searched for information about Sandy Wills. He immediately found valuable information from U. S. government records from the 1800s, including census, military, and pension data available at the National Archives, which is a federal organization that holds our country's historical and governmental records. I was shocked when Craig emailed me right away and said, "Guess what? Sandy Wills is your great-great-great grandfather, and a slave owner named Edmund Wills purchased him at auction in about 1850, when he was only ten years old!" My jaw dropped.

Wow, thanks to the Internet, a smart researcher, and a lot of luck, another Wills man seemed to be coming home to us, Grandpa Sandy Wills! But I wanted and needed to know more. Even with so much information online, finding any accurate data about slaves and their families was difficult. Slaves were not treated as human beings. They were bought and sold so haphazardly in the United States that researching accurate family connections was difficult. Also, the people who created the census—a list of U. S. citizens—kept track of how many slaves American citizens owned, but the census did not report the names of slaves. They were only listed by their estimated ages and by gender. Imagine that—not even their birthdays were known!

Curiously, slaves were also distinguished as either "black" or "mulatto," meaning of mixed race, probably because mulatto slaves fetched more money at the slave auctions. And slaves were usually given the last names of their owners, which could change with every sale of their priceless souls. A person today would have to be lucky, very lucky, to be able to identify his or her slave ancestors.

But luck was on our side this time as census records had information on Grandpa Sandy because he returned to Haywood County, Tennessee, even after slavery was abolished after the end of the Civil War in 1865. For generations, Grandpa Sandy's children, along with his children's children, all married legally and lived in Haywood County—and thus kept the Wills name and bloodline intact. In fact, in 1942, my very own father was among the last of Grandpa Sandy's great-great grandchildren born in Haywood County.

Mostly, though, we got lucky because Grandpa Sandy had Grandma Emma as his wife. She later applied in 1900 for a pension from the U.S. government because her husband, Grandpa Sandy, was a soldier in the U.S. Army. In applying for a pension, she had to provide very detailed and accurate information in hundreds of pages of records proving her right to receive a pension. This information is stored in the National Archives today. Thanks to Grandma Emma, we were able to bring Grandpa Sandy and others in my family back to life. Go, Grandma Emma!

Like many African Americans, I had always assumed that I was a descendant of Africans who were held as slaves, but this was certainly the first time that I had pinpointed a specific ancestor. I was humbled. The information was overwhelming. I was shocked to have identified a great-great-great-grandfather who was born a slave. And I was sickened, too, to learn that he was sold to a new owner at ten years of age! But I was also very proud when research revealed that Grandpa Sandy was later a soldier in the Civil War from 1863 to 1865 and that he fought against slavery! Unbelievable! I felt like American royalty and still do. My siblings and I are all proud to know that we had an ancestor who had a direct hand in ending slavery! Not many Americans can say that.

Wills Family Archives

My father, Clarence Wills, was a brave and proud member of the New York City Fire Department.

Wills Family Archives

In 1956, Grandpa Fred, well-dressed as always, visited the Statue of Liberty in New York City.
73
UE OF LIBERTY
1956
N.Y.

Wills Family Archives

Grandma Opal was the rock of the Wills family. Practical yet romantic, she eloped to Mississippi with Grandpa Fred in 1941.

Wills Family Archives

Even as a young boy in Haywood County, Tennessee, my dad (third from left) stood apart from others in our family.

Wills Family Archives

Grandpa Fred was a proud father with two sons who loved him deeply.

Wills Family Archives

Both dad and Uncle Van (left) learned to play the guitar at a young age, inspired by both gospel and soul music.

Wills Family Archives

In the mid-1950s, my dad enjoyed exploring New York City with his best friend Frankie.

Wills Family Archives

My mother (center) smiled next to Grandma Sallie and Grandpa Hardy. They were loving but strict parents.

Wills Family Archives

A brave paratrooper in the U.S. Army, my dad enjoyed the sense of freedom he felt when jumping from airplanes.

Wills Family Archives

In 1965, my dad married the love of his life, my mom.

Wills Family Archives

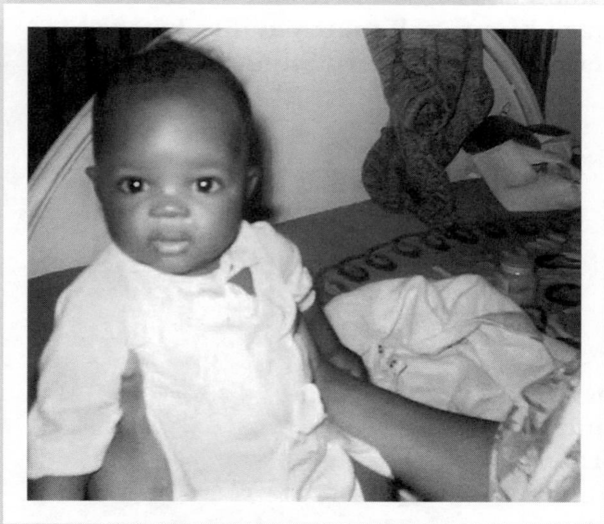

I was a happy baby, excited to be the center of attention.

Wills Family Archives

Grandpa Fred was known throughout the neighborhood as the "Candyman." Children often begged him to sell them candies before church services began every Sunday.

Wills Family Archives

In 1974, my brother Big Boy and I celebrated my eighth birthday.

Wills Family Archives

We were a small family before my sisters and other brother were born.

Wills Family Archives

I barely smiled because I was constantly worried about my dad.

Wills Family Archives

My dad was one of the first black firemen to join the famous firehouse, Engine 1, Ladder 24, in New York City.

Wills Family Archives

We were one of the first families to move into a new gated community called Ocean Village, located next to the beach in The Rockaways, New York City.

Wills Family Archives

This photo was taken from our apartment window. My dad loved his motorcycle.

Wills Family Archives

This is the last photo of my dad ever taken. He was no longer a caring, attentive father.

Wills Family Archives

I was unhappy to see members of my dad's motorcycle club, the New Comers, at his funeral.

Wills Family Archives

An honor guard from the New York City Fire Department carried my dad's coffin into the church on September 11, 1980.

Wills Family Archives

Following my dad's death, our family struggled. I was in too much pain to smile.

Wills Family Archives

My dad died too young. His life was full of great successes and tragic failures.

CHAPTER FOUR

Making the Invisible Visible

I live to make the invisible visible,
To show how once upon a nightmare,
beautiful, innocent people
were reduced to ghosts.
The United Shadows of America, they were.
To be seen, but not heard.
To work, but not be compensated.
To die, but not be remembered.

Slave owner Edmund Willis Wills gave me my family name, but he was no relative of mine, believe me! His plantation in Haywood County, Tennessee, was essentially a prison for Grandpa Sandy. No movie can ever fully capture the horrors of slavery in our great nation from the 1600s to the 1800s. Male and female slaves of all shapes and sizes lived on the Wills plantation, some tall, others short, all hailing from diverse African tribes and ethnic groups. Their skin pigments were of every hue of brown—falling between boot-black and cotton-ball white, between cafe au lait and butter pecan.

Their complexions formed a rainbow of colored castaways. No matter what their color was, though, they were all dyed-in-the-wool, red-blooded Americans whether the Constitution recognized them as such or not. These slaves stood united in their hope to have a system that did not strip them of their humanity and their liberty. They were not educated, but they were not stupid either.

Slave owner Edmund Wills was born in 1805 in Virginia. His parents had owned slaves. This life was the only one that Edmund knew. When Edmund came of age, he moved his wife, children, extended family, and—most important—his slaves away from Virginia to Haywood County, Tennessee, where the local black population easily outnumbered the white population. The area was rural, with a population of about seventeen thousand people in 1850.

The Wills family moved to Haywood County to grow cotton, as it was the nation's largest export. Edmund and his wife, Harriet Yancey, who was born in 1814 in Virginia, had nine children: Eliza, Sarah, John, Maria, William, Hibirnia, Caledonia, Edmund, and Frances. The Wills children all attended school and lived comfortably on their plantation thanks to the blood, sweat, and tears of enslaved African men and women.

Throughout the 1840s and 1850s, the harsh man widely known in the area as Master Wills proved to be successful in the business of buying and selling human beings. An ambitious although misguided soul, Master Wills became one of the largest slaveholders in Haywood County. Just to be clear, the average price for the sale of a slave in 1850 was about $400, the same as the cost of the average house in our nation at that time. Today, that same $400 from 1850 would be worth about $12,000.

Blinded by ambition and greed, slave traders like Edmund Wills forgot the lessons gained during the fight for American independence against the British in the 1700s, and perhaps in forgetting these lessons, the slaveholders increased their brutish ways. Edmund Wills and his parents were direct beneficiaries of a fierce battle for liberty and freedom and yet used their newfound independence to oppress vulnerable people like those in my family. Unbelievable!

According to the 1860 U.S. Census Slave Schedule, forty-eight slaves lived on the Wills plantation. In some ways, Master Wills could be considered a rich man. In most ways, however, I consider him to be a man with an impoverished heart and a bankrupt soul. The most haunting aspect of the Census Slave Schedule is that it lists only the number of slaves Edmund owned—but nothing about their identities. Seriously, it's as if the slaves were ghosts. No names or family ties are cited. Each slave is listed first by age, next by sex, and then by *b* for black or *m* for mulatto. That's all! Sandy is not explicitly named, but he is one of two ten-year-old black males listed. Six other slaves were designated as *mulatto*. Why this description mattered in the life of a slave is unclear. Perhaps the label *mulatto* confirmed what many knew but would not feel safe talking about: Many white masters and overseers also had children with their black female slaves.

Grandpa Sandy Wills was born on a slave plantation in about 1840 in Tipton County, Tennessee, a small farming town just about twenty-seven miles west of

Haywood County. It, too, was full of plantations with black slaves. The quiet community gently kissed the Mississippi River just north of the big city, Memphis, about thirty-one miles away.

Grandpa Sandy likely entered this world in an unsanitary, dark, and cramped shack. Bloodied and soiled sheets were crumpled beneath his exhausted slave mother, a woman whom history would quickly forget. Those in attendance at Grandpa Sandy's birth probably welcomed the infant with a sad joy, knowing that the child had just departed the only free world he would ever know: his mother's womb. Grandpa Sandy's dark future had already been predetermined; he was born into a barbarous and brutal universe where he'd be forced to work when he wanted to rest and to laugh when he wanted to cry. Grandpa Sandy's loving mother, whose name we will likely never know, may have screamed in agony, not only for the excruciating and debilitating pain of childbirth, but also for the unbearable life her little bundle of joy would be forced to endure in the years ahead.

The cruelest irony was that upon hearing of Grandpa Sandy's successful delivery, his mother's slave master was likely beside himself with joy. As a harsh businessman, he calculated that the healthy newborn would grow into a strong young man and provide a lucrative return on Master's human investment.

No one bothered to write down the exact date on which Grandpa Sandy was born. Who cared? Slaves worked, and then they died—they were not expected to be memorable or to contribute anything meaningful to the world. In a nation that prided itself on literacy and recordkeeping, slaves were not taught to read or write because education has always meant power. Slave owners had a vested interest in keeping slaves ignorant and powerless. However, the date of Grandpa Sandy's entry into the United States of America was significant because he was among the last few generations of colored children born into the wicked cycle of slavery.

In 1850, Grandpa Sandy was ten years old when he was dressed and prepared for sale after being taken away from his mom forever. A dreaded bell tolled for his transaction. I find it hard to believe that such horrors actually happened in our country. Here's how one slave described seeing the terrible sorrow of a female slave after her husband and children were all sold to different buyers at a slave auction: "With all our care, we lost one woman who had been taken from her husband and children, and having no desire to live without them, in the agony of her soul jumped overboard and drowned herself."[1]

When Edmund Wills saw young Sandy for sale at the slave auction, Sandy's dark-brown skin, gleaming in the Tennessee sun, must have clearly impressed the Master. Sandy was a strong and able boy. As was customary, Master Wills likely hoped that his new slave would prove to be not too intelligent. Like many other slave owners, Master Wills perhaps knew that an intelligent slave might seek to run away because of a strong "love for freedom, patriotism, insurrection, bloodshed, and…war against American slavery."[2]

Life for Sandy was insufferable, as it was for all slaves. They worked hard from dawn to dusk six days a week. A typical day of work lasted 12–15 hours.

Sundays were often days of rest. The only holidays that slaves had off from work were Christmas and July 4! Male and female slaves worked either in the fields or in their master's house. Field slaves farmed the land under the hot sun for a variety of crops, including cotton, sugar, rice, and tobacco. House slaves worked in their master's house and were responsible for cooking, cleaning, washing clothes, and taking care of the master's family. Slave children were not taught to read and write. They were legally prohibited from attending school, and they could not be homeschooled. Masters knew that literacy would eventually lead to liberty for the slaves. Children's work included cleaning, carrying water to the fields, taking care of animals and gardens, and caring for younger slave children.

Slaves typically lived all cramped together in dilapidated wooden shacks with little protection from rain, snow, or scorching summer heat. A fireplace was the center of life in the house, providing fire for both cooking at mealtime and warmth during cold months. Beds were made of straw. Floors were dirty and made of mud. The shacks often lacked windows and were very hot in the summer and very cold in the winter.

A slave described his home as follows:

> Us never had a chair in the house. My Pa made benches for us to site [sic] by the fire on.... We had a large plank table that Pa made. Never had no mirrors. Went to [the] spring to see ourselves on a Sunday morning. Never had...dressers in them days. All us had was a table, benches, and beds. And my Pa made them.[3]

Slaves ate two meals a day, breakfast, and then later in the night, dinner. They were given minimal amounts of food. Their diet varied and included cornmeal, pork, and salt herring. Some also ate beef, possum, rabbits, and fish. Others had plenty of sugar, syrup, and flour.

In the same year that Grandpa Sandy was sold into slavery to Master Wills, tensions were brewing around the nation between those who wanted slavery to exist and those who surely didn't. The 1850 Fugitive Slave Law angered abolitionists like Frederick Douglass and John Brown. This appalling law gave federal agents the power to recover slaves who had escaped to the North, and it disregarded the rights of free blacks who were captured by slave hunters. At about the same time, antislavery activist John Brown wrote, "The Fugitive Slave Law was to be the means of making more Abolitionists than all the lectures we have had for years."[4] The country's tension was a firestorm in the making.

Soon after moving to the Wills plantation in 1850, Grandpa Sandy bonded with five young slave boys: Mack Wills, Richard Wills, James Wills, Andy Wills, and Dick Wills. They were all owned by Master Wills and were not brothers by blood, but they were brothers in bondage. On a slave plantation, bondage was thicker than blood. Grandpa Sandy was about five years older than the other boys, so when he spoke, the younger ones likely listened and obeyed him. As their baby teeth fell out and their adult teeth grew in, Grandpa Sandy was probably the one to organize the innocent games that the boys played throughout the wide-open plantation fields. A game they may have played was called "Hide the Switch." One of the boys would hide a switch, a tree branch, and whoever found it would then chase the other boys and try to whip them. More than one hundred years later, far away in New York City, my friends and I played the very same game, but we called it "Hot Peas and Butter."

Grandpa Sandy, the tallest among the boys, also likely fetched the sweetest fruit from the tallest trees for his younger, hungry brothers. As they lay on their backs and looked up at the deep blue sky, I bet each boy dreamed of flying toward the clouds high above and being forever free.

For Grandpa Sandy, time spent with his brothers offered great relief from the horrors of slavery. The boys were all far removed from their families. These brothers in bondage had only each other to protect and nurture their young souls. Sometimes, though, the boys couldn't protect each other as each of them experienced ruthless beatings for disobedience or for attempting to escape. Dear Grandpa Sandy's broad, strong back was probably scarred by the lashes of his master's bullwhip, a punishment surely designed to instill dreadful fear into his pure heart. In the simple equation of right and wrong, Grandpa Sandy no doubt judged slavery wrong. In the equation of just and unjust, Grandpa Sandy deemed slavery unjust. In the equation of life and death, he clearly reasoned that life equaled freedom. Slavery meant death.

Slavery was not only a physical bondage, but also a mental one. Many slaves were religious, and they did not want to anger their God. Conditioned and brainwashed not only to obey their owners but also to love them as well, slaves were taught that the Bible told them that Master's word was law. Masters also taught slaves that their sole purpose in life was to work hard to make profits for others, not for themselves. While cruel slave owners used every trick in the book to keep Grandpa Sandy and millions of other slaves in check, they could not blind their slaves' eyes, they could not mute their ears, and they could not, try as they might, break their spirits.

When Grandpa Sandy turned twenty-one in 1861, he surely heard talk of secession, as one Southern state after another left the United States to form a new country, the Confederate States of America. Grandpa Sandy, like most slaves, reckoned that a war between the states would be strictly about his freedom. Few whites in Tennessee would make that assertion, but blacks and abolitionists accepted that idea as fact. Sandy may not have been able to write about how a war might set him and his so-called brothers free, but he didn't need an education to know right from wrong. Armed with that conviction, Sandy didn't need to know "nuth'in" else. However, many whites saw the fight as a battle over state governance or independence, with the Southern states upset by the too far-reaching actions of the federal government.

On November 6, 1860, a Northerner named Abraham Lincoln was elected president of the United States. His election outraged many people in the South. A few months later, in April 1861, the Confederates attacked Fort Sumter in Charleston, South Carolina. The Union troops inside the fort fired back. The Civil War had begun.

CHAPTER FIVE

The Sounds of Freedom

War was the sweetest sound
to that slave named Sandy.
The poor soul had never known a day of peace.
The sound of gunfire was like
Angels singing the sweet song of redemption.
The war within …
was finally turned inside out.
Brother against brother!
Sandy was caught in the crossfire,
And bullets were such sweet sorrow.

By 1861, the Civil War had started as Union soldiers from the North fought against their Confederate enemies from the South. By 1862, slaves in the fields throughout the South could hear the Confederate soldiers' terrifying battle cry, "Yee Haw," echoing throughout the countryside. This rebel yell was a deep, frightening howl meant to energize the Confederate troops and instill terror into the Union soldiers who were trespassing upon Southern soil.

As uniformed soldiers spilled their blood on Tennessee soil, nearby slaves likely roared a silent rebel yell of their own, coming from deep within their hearts. Their growl captured the deep agony and humiliation of generations of slaves. As Americans pierced each other's flesh and turned Tennessee fields into burial grounds, slaves, including Grandpa Sandy, bided their time. They hoped—and perhaps knew—that the clock would soon strike midnight for slavery.

At first, Grandpa Sandy's vantage point of the war was limited to the Wills plantation in Haywood County. He could not see the Union soldiers attacking cities and towns in Tennessee, but he could feel the rumblings of change in the air. Yet even as the Union soldiers destroyed railroad tracks and burned plantations to the ground, slave owners like Edmund Wills still had absolutely no intention of relocating their families and human property from Haywood County.

Grandpa Sandy, though, and many other slaves had their own ideas about "business as usual." At the beginning of the war, many free black men in the North wanted to join in the fight against the Confederates in the South. The former slave Frederick Douglass, who had become a famous abolitionist leader before the war, stated, "We are ready and would go."[5] Without a doubt, many slaves, including Grandpa Sandy, had somehow gotten wind of Douglass's unwavering appeal to have slaves join the Union Army. President Lincoln initially resisted Douglass's idea. Lincoln had long insisted that the war was not about freeing the slaves; instead, he maintained, it was more about saving the nation. In 1862, Lincoln stated his goal for the war: "I would save the Union.... If I could save the Union without freeing any slave, I would do it, and I if could save it by freeing all the slaves, I would do it.... What I do about Slavery and the colored race, I do because I believe it helps to save this Union."[6]

After more than a year of bloody war, President Lincoln issued the Emancipation Proclamation on September 22, 1862. In the proclamation, which took effect on January 1, 1863, Lincoln declared "that all persons held as slaves [within the rebellious states] are, and henceforward shall be free."[7] Tennessee was exempt and not named in the proclamation because the state had mostly returned to Union control. So Grandpa Sandy and many thousands of slaves in Tennessee were left in limbo. They were still slaves in a Confederate state that was controlled by the Union, and they would remain slaves until the full surrender of the Confederacy and passage of the Thirteenth Amendment in 1865. As a result of the proclamation, the focus of the war shifted. The main goal of the war was now to free the slaves.

The proclamation also declared that black men could join the Union Army and Navy, finally enabling the so-called liberated "to become the liberators." In October 1862, African Americans first fought in battle against the Confederates at Island Mound, Missouri. Initially, many white people doubted the ability of black men to be effective soldiers. However, wherever they fought, black soldiers proved to be brave and skilled. In early 1863, President Lincoln stated, "The colored population is the great available...force for restoring the Union."[8]

In the same year, 1862, black leaders like Frederick Douglass tried to recruit black soldiers into the Union

Army. Sign-ups for black soldiers were slow at first, but volunteers soon joined as they were given an opportunity to become full citizens of the Union. In May 1863, the Union government established the Bureau of Colored Troops to manage the increasing numbers of black soldiers. Thanks to Douglass's efforts, many eligible blacks, including runaway slaves, signed up to serve. These regiments of black soldiers became known as the United States Colored Troops (USCT). In all, about 200,000 men joined the USCT. At long last, black men could become soldiers with the Union Army and fight for their freedom!

Some Americans, though, thought that allowing black men to become soldiers was a bad idea. These Americans just couldn't imagine seeing former slaves carrying rifles and dressed in blue military uniforms.

Nevertheless, for Grandpa Sandy, "business as usual" changed. He and his band of brothers now could put in place a daring plan that would change their lives forever. On or about August 22, 1863, Mack, Richard, James, and Andy Wills escaped from the Wills plantation in Haywood County. Boldly and bravely, they ventured into what they knew would be a very different life. If the four brothers somehow managed to make it safely to Fort Halleck in Columbus, Kentucky, they were prepared to join the Union Army and fight to the death to end slavery forever.

The four young brothers left Haywood County with nothing but rags on their backs. They probably did not even have shoes on their feet for the eighty-two mile walk from Haywood County to Fort Halleck in Columbus. How these illiterate slaves—who had never roamed freely before and couldn't read a map—knew exactly where they were going is unclear. Each step along the way could certainly have been their last. Perhaps slave catchers or Confederate soldiers were hot on their trail.

Finally, about five days later—on August 27, 1863—the brothers reached Fort Halleck, home to the 4th U. S. Colored Heavy Artillery Regiment. Their first order of business was perhaps to be interviewed by the enlistment officer, Lt. G.W. Fitterman.

First, Lt. Fitterman called on Mack Wills and carefully read each question from the army enlistment form he held in his hands.

Mack was asked to state his name. "My name is Mack Wills," he replied.

When asked his age, Mack said, "Eighteen."

Of course, he didn't really know his exact age or birthday. Next, an assistant may have used a measuring tape to determine Mack's height, which was listed as five feet, six inches. Lt. Fitterman probably didn't even bother to look deeply into Mack's eyes when writing that Mack had black eyes, black hair, and a black complexion. In actuality, Mack's skin was probably deep brown. Why would a white army officer care to be accurate about the color of a black man's skin? Everything in Lt. Fitterman's world was either black or white.

When asked where he was born, Mack replied, "Nashville, Tennessee."

The most startling and downright repulsive part of the entire interview was when Mack was asked to identify his occupation.

"Slave," he replied.

Upon first reading that word on Mack's enlistment form during my research, I couldn't breathe. I just couldn't peel my eyes away from the words, *Occupation: slave.* I asked myself, *Was slavery really a normal occupation?* Slavery is many things, but one thing it is not—it is NOT an occupation. To make matters worse, in the remarks section of the form, Lt. Fitterman added, "Owned by Edmund Wills, Haywood Co. Tenn."

One insight was very clear to me as I read and reviewed Mack's enlistment form. Slavery was disastrous not only for blacks, but also for slaveholders. Slaveholders had lost all sense of decency and compassion for people with different-colored skin. That a distinguished Union officer in uniform could calmly write down on an official form that another human being was a slave still stuns me. For sure, slavery is a condition he most certainly would not have accepted for himself or his own children. Yet his writing something like "not applicable" would have been preferable. *Occupation: Slave* is yet another disturbing footnote in the annals of our nation's history.

Next up for an interview with Lt. Fitterman was James Wills.

"James Wills, sir," James quickly responded when asked his name.

The drill was probably the same. The enlistment officer noted that James stood five feet, eight inches tall. James, like Mack, was also just a few months shy of his eighteenth birthday. James was the younger biological brother of Dick Wills. Unlike the rest of the boys, James and Dick were able to identify their parents, Dick Parker and Caroline Parker, both of whom were presumably born sometime in the 1820s.

Next, Lt. Fitterman noted that James's hair, eyes, and complexion were black. Once again, the lieutenant jotted down the disheartening classification on the enlistment form: "slave, owned by Edmund Wills, Haywood Co Tenn."

Next up: "Haywood County, sir" was where Richard Wills said he was born.

Lt. Fitterman documented that Richard was eighteen years old and stood five feet, six and a half inches. Lt. Fitterman then wrote, "black," to describe Richard's complexion, eyes, and hair.

Next up: "Andy Wills, sir," Andy Wills replied when asked his name.

Lt. Fitterman then noted that Andy was five feet, five inches tall.

"I don't know, sir," Andy simply responded when asked where he was born.

Andy was the only brother who admitted that he didn't know when he was born or from where he came. He could've made up a town, but he didn't. He was honest. His response was brief and probably passed without much notice, but his unsettling response was devastating. For all Andy knew, he had sprung up out of the ground from nowhere, just like a turnip seed.

Of all the boys, Andy was the one closest to Grandpa Sandy. In a general affidavit filed after the war, Andy testified that he had even slept in the same shack as Grandpa Sandy when they were slave children. He was just nine years old when he met

Grandpa Sandy. While Andy did not know his past at all, he could easily envision his future as a soldier fighting for the Union.

And where were Grandpa Sandy and Dick Wills? The oldest among the brothers, they did not escape with the others to Fort Halleck. Why they remained at the plantation is unclear. That they were afraid to run away with the others is highly doubtful. Perhaps they stayed behind to make sure Master Wills did not hire slave catchers with dogs to sniff out and capture the four runaways in the middle of the night. Possibly, Grandpa Sandy and Dick wanted to take the punishment for the others' escape rather than allow another slave to reveal their escape plan while under duress during a beating at the whipping post. Or maybe Grandpa Sandy even lied to Master Wills and assured him that Mack, James, Richard, and Andy would soon return to the plantation. Many possible scenarios exist, none of which have been recorded in any of the documents that I researched.

Probably, however, Grandpa Sandy and Dick Wills were savagely beaten within an inch of their lives for helping the brothers to escape. The two of them were obviously close to the four runaways, especially to Andy. Master Wills probably reasoned that Grandpa Sandy and Dick had helped plan the escape. For Master Wills, the loss of the slaves meant the loss of profits from their work. They were prized slaves: young, strong, and able to father younger slaves to then be sold for profit.

If Grandpa Sandy and Dick were punished, possibly they were "staked out," a common method of torture for rebellious slaves. Four stakes were driven into the ground, and each slave's arms and legs were tied to a stake. The overseer, or perhaps Edmund Wills himself, may have wielded a paddle and thrashed the soles of the victim's feet until each foot was bloody and raw. In a final act of cruelty, the torturer would then whip out a knife and slash the bloodied foot blisters to prevent the slave from running away.

Perhaps these barbarians had other ideas for punishing Grandpa Sandy and Dick. The boys could have been stripped and tied to a tree and mercilessly whipped with anything that was available—from wooden switches to leather strips. Perhaps Grandpa Sandy and Dick were "bucked." That is, their feet were tied together and their knees were pushed up to their chins. Then their hands were tied together over their knees. Lastly, a stick or rod was then shoved under their legs and over their arms. Victims remained bound in this painful position for hours.

No matter what happened to Grandpa Sandy and Dick following their brothers' escape, their plans never changed. About fifty days later, on October 11, 1863, Grandpa Sandy and Dick escaped and followed in the footsteps of Mack, James, Richard, and Andy. Dick walked the same eighty-two miles to Columbus, Kentucky, and enlisted with the same regiment that his brothers had joined.

Dick was likely a bit more defiant than his younger brothers. He proudly identified himself as Dick Parker when asked his name by the enlistment officer, Lt. Fitterman. Dick's legal last name was Wills, because he, like Grandpa Sandy, was the property of Edmund

Wills, but Dick never forgot that he was named for his father, Dick Parker. Even under the oppression of slavery, Dick had always embraced his biological father's identity.

Dick was rebellious for sure. I really love that he switched his name back to Parker! More than thirty years later, in an affidavit for his pension, he stated, "When a slave before the war I belonged to Edmund Willis Wills who raised me, therefore [I] was known as Dick Wills, but after the War I took the name of my father Dick Parker. I was named for him and have always been named Dick Parker."[9]

Bam! Dick essentially said, "I reject the name Edmund Wills—he can have it back! Now I'm in control, and the first thing I'm reclaiming is my name!" Every time I think about Dick Parker, I give him a virtual high five! He had guts!

Lt. Fitterman entered Dick's name on the enlistment form as Dick Parker, unaware of Dick's courageous act of reclaiming his original name. This first warning shot from Dick Parker indicated that the war over slavery had already been won. Lt. Fitterman also noted that Dick was twenty-two years old and was five feet, four and a half inches tall. His complexion, eyes, and hair color were deemed black. Dick later described his skin color as dark ginger cake, which was a popular dessert that could easily be mistaken for chocolate cake until you tasted the finely chopped fresh ginger, black pepper, and cinnamon. Dick's characterization of his bronze skin was certainly more creative than Lt. Fitterman's description. The lieutenant never would have associated a delicious piece of cake with a person of African descent. Apparently, Dick Parker viewed himself as one of the sweeter things in life, and he was right.

Dick went on to tell Lt. Fitterman that he was born in Haywood County, Tennessee, and had belonged to Edmund Wills. Like all of the other Wills men, he had signed up to serve a five-year term as a soldier, assuming the horrible war lasted that long. To my delight, the occupation section on Dick's enlistment form was left blank. Lt. Fitterman did not identify Dick as "slave" as he did the other Wills men. Why Lt. Fitterman left this section blank is unclear. Could Dick have told him outright to leave it blank? I wouldn't put it past him! Perhaps Lt. Fitterman finally realized that classifying slavery as an occupation was absurd!

Unlike his brother, Grandpa Sandy enlisted in the Union Army at Union City, Tennessee, on October 13, 1863. Union City was more than twenty miles from Fort Halleck and about seventy miles from Haywood County. Why Grandpa Sandy chose to enlist at that location is unclear.

During his enlistment, Grandpa Sandy stood alone before the enlistment officer, Lt. J.S. Mauggy.

"My name is Sandy Willis Wills," Grandpa Wills proudly said.

Lt. Mauggy apparently misunderstood Grandpa Sandy and wrote his name on the enlistment form as "Sandy Willis." This simple written error would lead to great frustration in the years following the war.

As Grandpa Sandy faced his enlistment officer, he stated his age as twenty-three years old and said he was born in Tipton County, which was about twenty-seven miles west of Haywood County. Then probably without ever even raising his head to look at Grandpa Sandy, Lt. Mauggy wrote "blk" to describe his complexion, eyes, and hair color. Grandpa Sandy's height was then noted as well—five feet, nine and a half inches.

Then when it came to identifying Grandpa Sandy's occupation, the officer simply wrote, "Farmer." That designation seemed strange to me and really caught my attention. Maybe Grandpa Sandy told Lt. Mauggy that he was a slave and the officer wrote, "Farmer," on the enlistment form. That scenario seems unlikely. Perhaps Grandpa Sandy took his own action and described his occupation as a farmer. If that's true, then Grandpa Sandy was far more liberated and more revolutionary than I could have possibly imagined. If Grandpa Sandy uttered, "farmer," he did not allow the forces of slavery, mighty as they were, to define him. If Grandpa Sandy declared himself essentially a free man who made his living as a farmer, then that claim proves that he, too, had fought and won the war long before he actually put on a blue Union uniform. Also, Grandpa Sandy's enlistment form did not include anything to indicate that he was "owned by Edmund Wills of Haywood County." Whoa! That omission is probably because Grandpa Sandy instinctively knew that despite evidence to the contrary, he could not be bought. His soul was not for sale.

So they made it! Grandpa Sandy, Mack, James, Richard, Andy, and Dick were now privates in the U.S. Army. At first, the colored regiments were exclusively led by white officers, but as the war waged on, a handful of black soldiers were promoted to be officers as well. Initially, black soldiers earned less money than white ones. They were paid $7 per month, with a charge of $3 for clothing. On the other hand, white soldiers were paid $13 per month, with an additional $3.50 clothing allowance. Later, after much dissension and national outcry, black soldiers were granted equal pay in 1864.

As the war raged on, these brave new soldiers likely faced many challenges. The feisty and illiterate new recruits were issued one hundred bullets, but they did not know how to count to one hundred. Black soldiers on the move who came upon signs in the street couldn't read the signs. When paid, they could not understand the value of the money they received.

As a member of the USCT, Grandpa Sandy and his brothers had many eye-opening experiences. For the first time, they wore shoes and uniforms. During their training, newbies were handed muskets and revolvers and taught how to aim at a target and pull a gun trigger. Also, a looming question surfaced: Could the black soldiers be trained to kill white people whom they had been forced to love and serve as slaves?

Sadly, tragedy struck the brothers before the first bullet was ever fired at them. Richard Wills got sick during training exercises. The young soldier fell gravely ill just four months after he enlisted in the Union Army. Without warning, his body became wracked with pain. He developed a cough that wouldn't quit. With a high fever and bloodshot eyes, he was taken to the hospital where he was immediately diagnosed with measles, or rubeola as it was sometimes called at the time. Richard was struggling to stay alive. When his comrades last saw him, they prayed that he would live until the end of the war. Unfortunately, Richard's health did not improve. As death hung in the air, the young men likely reflected on their childhoods with Richard and remembered the precious few joys they had all shared together. Richard's condition soon grew worse. Five days before Christmas, on December 20, 1863, Richard Wills, brother, risk-taker, and soldier, died.

While researching Richard's death, I often wondered what had happened to his remains. Certainly, slave master Edmund Wills didn't want them as Richard was of no use to him as a dead person. The institution of slavery had erased Richard's heritage and robbed him of his birthright. As a slave, he had always been a ghost—a dead man walking—with no firm identity, no independence, and no legacy.

Richard's death was an inspiration. Perhaps his brothers honored his life with a small, intimate funeral. Someone must have reminisced about the summer days when young Richard and the boys would sneak away and lie on their backs, admiring the birds flying free up in the sky.

His brothers may have viewed his death not as a crushing blow, but as a solid victory. Richard didn't get to fight in this brutal war, but he did fly high and get a taste of freedom. As harrowing as Richard's short eighteen years had been, he died a free man.

Department of Veterans Affairs

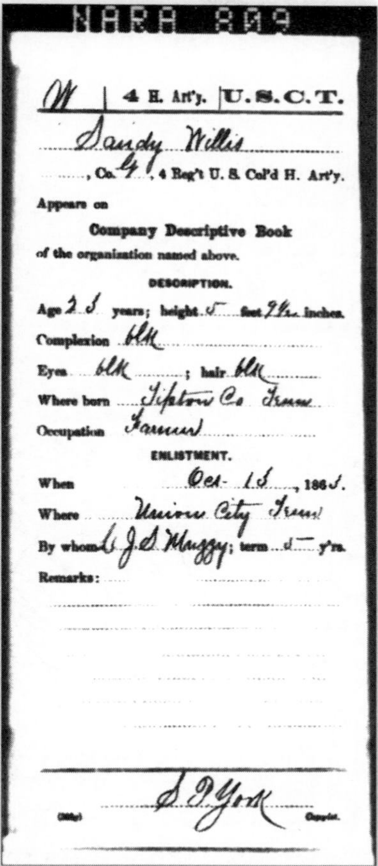

NARA 809

W | 4 H. Art'y. | U.S.C.T.

Sandy Willis

, Co. G, 4 Reg't U. S. Col'd H. Art'y.

Appears on

Company Descriptive Book

of the organization named above.

DESCRIPTION.

Age 23 years; height 5 feet 9½ inches.

Complexion blk

Eyes blk ; hair blk

Where born Tipton Co Tenn

Occupation Farmer

ENLISTMENT.

When Oct 13, 1863.

Where Union City Tenn

By whom Lt J S Muzzy; term 3 y'rs.

Remarks:

S. P. York

(368y) Copyist.

Department of Veterans Affairs

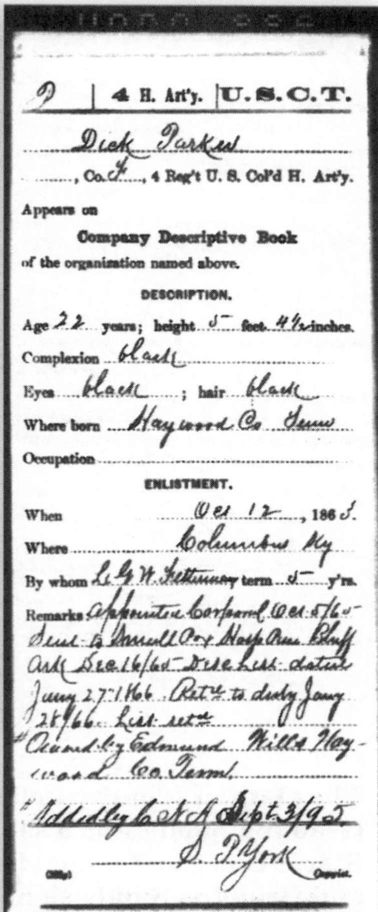

P | 4 H. Art'y. | U.S.C.T.

Dick Parker

, Co. F, 4 Reg't U. S. Col'd H. Art'y.

Appears on

Company Descriptive Book

of the organization named above.

DESCRIPTION.

Age 22 years; height 5 feet 4½ inches.

Complexion black

Eyes black ; hair black

Where born Haywood Co Tenn

Occupation

ENLISTMENT.

When Oct 12, 1863.

Where Columbus Ky

By whom Lt G W Fettinger term 3 y'rs.

Remarks Appointed Corporal Oct 5/65 Sent to ... Hosp Ark Bluff Ark Dec 16/65 Disc list dated Jany 27 1866. Ret'd to duty Jany 28/66. List ret'd.

Owned by Edmund Wills Haywood Co Tenn.

Noddley to N A Sept 3/95

S. P. York

(368y) Copyist.

In 1863, Sandy Wills (note his name is misspelled as "Willis") and Dick Parker enlisted in the United States Colored Troops.

Department of Veterans Affairs

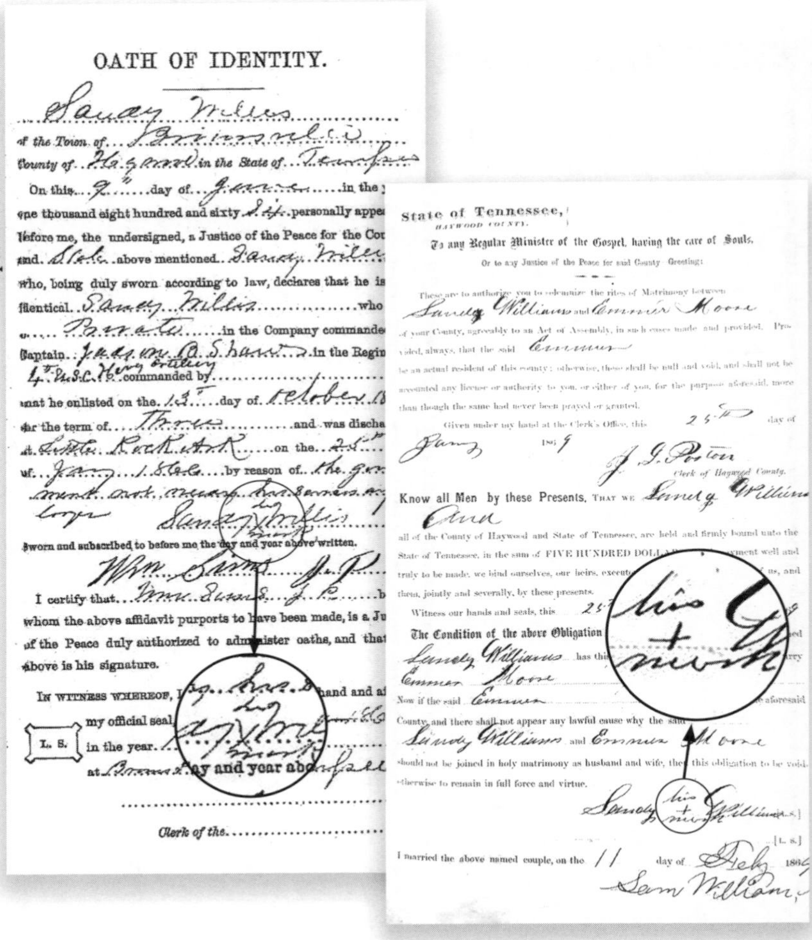

OATH OF IDENTITY.

Sandy Wills

of the Town of Brownsville

County of Haywood in the State of Tennessee

On this 9th day of June in the y[ear] one thousand eight hundred and sixty six personally appea[red] before me, the undersigned, a Justice of the Peace for the Co[unty] and State above mentioned Sandy Wills who, being duly sworn according to law, declares that he is [the] identical Sandy Willis who [was a] Private in the Company commande[d by] Captain Jackson A. Shaw in the Regi[ment] 4th U.S.C. Heavy Artillery commanded by ... that he enlisted on the 13th day of October 18... for the term of Three and was discha[rged] at Little Rock Ark on the 25th [day] of Jany 1866 by reason of the government not needing his services any longer

Sandy Willis [his mark]

Sworn and subscribed to before me the day and year above written.

Wm. Sims J.P.

I certify that Wm Sims J.P. b[efore] whom the above affidavit purports to have been made, is a Ju[stice] of the Peace duly authorized to administer oaths, and tha[t] above is his signature.

In witness whereof, I ... hand and a[ffixed] my official seal ... in the year ... at Brownsville day and year above ...

L. S.

Clerk of the ...

State of Tennessee,
Haywood County.

To any Regular Minister of the Gospel, having the care of Souls,
Or to any Justice of the Peace for said County—Greeting:

These are to authorize you to solemnize the rites of Matrimony between Sandy Williams and Emmer Moore of your County, agreeably to an Act of Assembly, in such cases made and provided. Provided, always, that the said Emmer be an actual resident of this county; otherwise, these shall be null and void, and shall not be accounted any license or authority to you, or either of you, for the purpose aforesaid, more than though the same had never been prayed or granted.

Given under my hand at the Clerk's Office, this 25th day of Jany 1869

J. G. Poston
Clerk of Haywood County.

Know all Men by these Presents, That we Sandy Williams and ...
all of the County of Haywood and State of Tennessee, are held and firmly bound unto the State of Tennessee, in the sum of FIVE HUNDRED DOLLA[RS] ... [pa]yment well and truly to be made, we bind ourselves, our heirs, execut[ors] ... us, and them, jointly and severally, by these presents.

Witness our hands and seals, this 25th ...

The Condition of the above Obligation ... Sandy Williams has this ... [ma]rry Emmer Moore

Now if the said Emmer ... aforesaid County, and there shall not appear any lawful cause why the said Sandy Williams and Emmer Moore should not be joined in holy matrimony as husband and wife, then this obligation to be void, otherwise to remain in full force and virtue.

Sandy his + mark Williams [L. S.]

[L. S.]

I married the above named couple, on the 11 day of Feby 1869

Sam Williams

Department of Veterans Affairs

The Oath of Identity (left) confirmed that Grandpa Sandy was a soldier with the United States Colored Troops. Both Grandma Emma and Grandpa Sandy signed their names with an *X*, because they could not read or write. As indicated in their marriage certificate (right), they were married on January 25, 1869. Note that his last name is mistakenly written as Williams, not Wills, due to a clerical error.

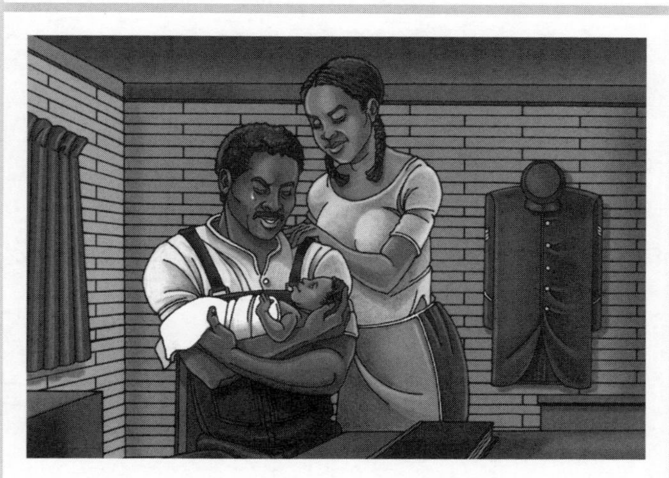

Illustrations from the book *The Emancipation of Grandpa Sandy Wills* depict Edmund Wills purchasing ten-year-old Sandy at a slave auction (top) in about 1850. In 1870, Grandpa Sandy and Grandma Emma (bottom) welcomed their first child.

Department of Veterans Affairs

3-446.

DEPOSITION A

Case of Emma Wills, No. 575,189

On this 6 day of March 1900, at Ged, county of Haywood, State of Tenn, before me, Geo A. Critchfield a special examiner of the Bureau of Pensions, personally appeared Emma Wills, who, being by me first duly sworn to answer truly all interrogatories propounded to her during this special examination of aforesaid claim for pension, deposes and says:

I am 49 years of age; my post-office address is Ged Tenn and I am by occupation a farmer. I am the identical Emma Wills who has made claim for pension as the widow of Sandy Wills who served during the Civil War ... States Army but I d... company or regiment ... in the same regiment ... Wills, Dick Parker, ... as he is sometimes calle... Cary Austin. ... I don't know any thin... of his enlistment ... He never served in but ... I never knew h... My said husband w... Wills and I never ... Sandy Willis except ... one who would misspe... He always said he w... as Sandy Wills and ... their name. His ow... Willie Wills. He is ... I got acquainted w... about two or three years ... He was always liv... in the neighborhood ... and after the war. I...

Page 5 Deposition A

Page 6

two miles and a half of here but I never happened to get acquainted with Sandy Wills until two or three years after the surrender though I knew his people.

Sandy Wills was never married before he married me and I was never married before I married him. I was about 17 or 18 years old when I married Sandy Wills. I married him by licence and there is a record of our marriage at Brownsville, Tenn. We were married by a colored methodist minister named Sam Williams who did live in Memphis Tenn a few years ago but two or three years ago I heard he was dead. We were married on the Moore place right in the Whitefolks house but the whitefolks were then living in Brownsville but Mr Joe Moore was there and saw us married as did also Nelson Moore who was one of our waiters. Elmira Moore his wife was there and Charley Bailey was there and many others who yet live around here.

I was married to Sandy Wills on Feb 11, 1869 as is shown by my Bible record which I show you. This record was made by Mr Joe Moore soon after we were married. All my children except one were born on his place and he also set the dates of their birth down in my bible as each one was born.

I had nine children by Sandy Wills eight of whom were living when he died and one was born the next month after he died. William our oldest child ...

Attest:
Bell Bond
William Wilkerson

Emma her x mark Wills
Deponent.

Sworn to and subscribed before me this 6 day of March, 1900, and I certify that the contents were fully made known to deponent before signing.

Geo A. Critchfield
Special Examiner.

Grandma Emma could not read or write, but she was forceful and disciplined as she provided depositions to the government to prove that she was eligible for a military pension after the death of Grandpa Sandy.

Ethan West

Ethan West

Cotton field (top) and former slave quarters (bottom) still exist today on the Moore plantation in Haywood County, Tennessee.

Ethan West

Mooreland is the name of the plantation where Grandma Emma and her family lived as slaves during the mid-1800s in Haywood County.

John Bertie Moore was the slavemaster who owned my Grandma Emma and her family.

Tennessee State Library and Archives

Wills Family Archives

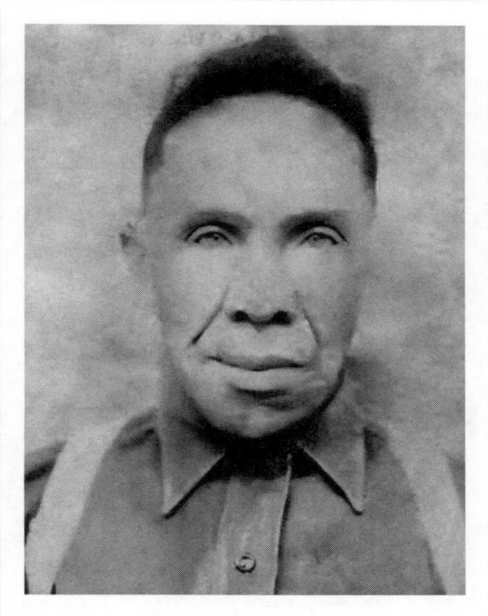

Grandpa Fred kept this photo of his father, Allen Wills, next to his bed for many years.

Ethan West

No records indicate where Grandma Emma and Grandpa Sandy were buried. Their graves might lie underneath this collapsed church in Haywood County.

I was honored to have Grandpa Fred walk me down the aisle in place of my dad at my wedding in 1994.

Wills Family Archives

Wills Family Archives

In 1991, Grandma Opal and Grandpa Fred renewed their vows at their fiftieth wedding anniversary party.

Wills Family Archives

Thirty years after my dad's death, we are still healing and can now smile again.

Wills Family Archives

My brother Big Boy and I hosted an event for people with special needs at the famed Apollo Theater in Harlem, New York City.

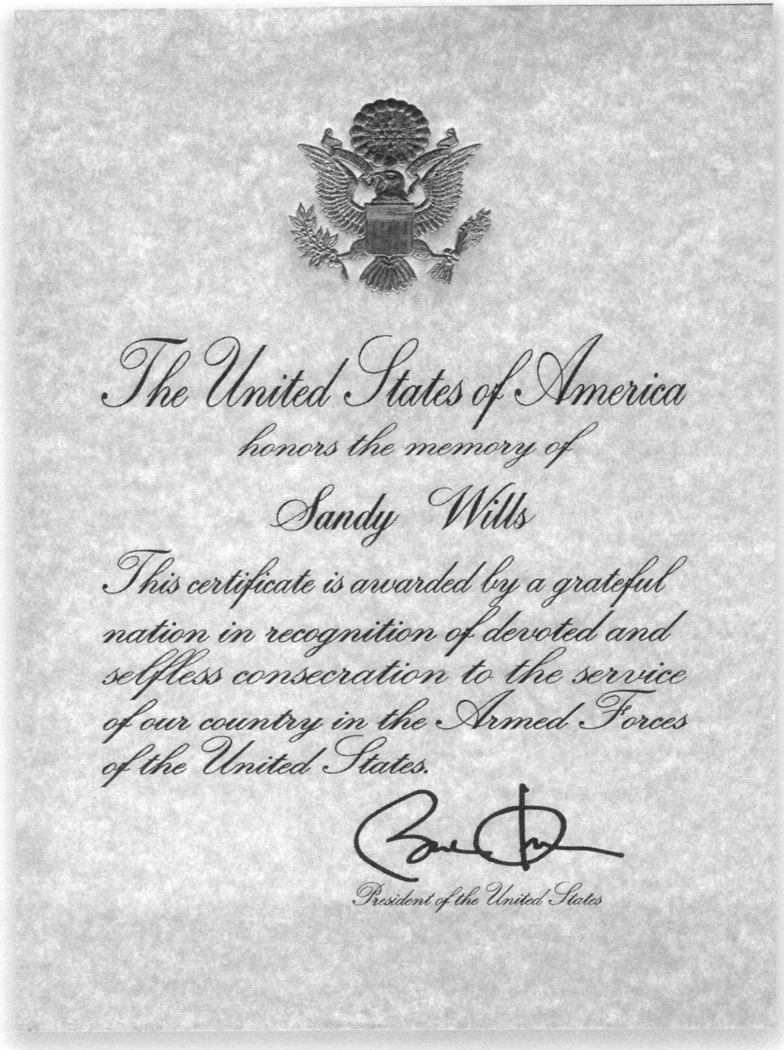

The United States of America
honors the memory of
Sandy Wills
This certificate is awarded by a grateful nation in recognition of devoted and selfless consecration to the service of our country in the Armed Forces of the United States.

President of the United States

Wills Family Archives

President Barack Obama signed this certificate to honor Grandpa Sandy's military service to our country during the Civil War.

Alonzo Boldin

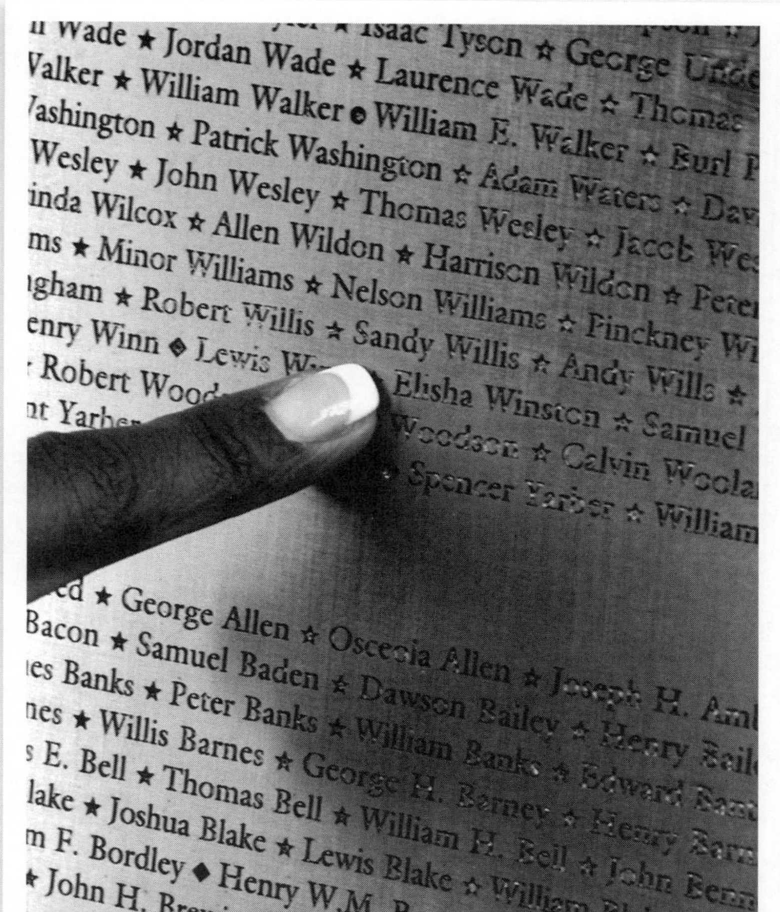

Grandpa Sandy's name is written on the wall (though misspelled as "Willis" as it appeared in his discharge papers) at the African American Civil War Memorial Museum in Washington, DC. The wall lists the names of soldiers, drawn from the records of the Bureau of United States Colored Troops at the National Archives.

CHAPTER SIX

Liberty Slayed Slavery

The death of slavery was liberty to thee.
Liberty slayed slavery to thee I sing.
Give me Liberty or Give me Death
Was the plea of the slave to his dying breath.
Patrick Henry said it first.
Grandpa Sandy proclaimed it, too.
Both men were patriots, but only one's history came through.

When my father and Uncle Van served as soldiers during the Vietnam War era in the 1960s, they were completely unaware that they were marching in some very powerful footsteps. One hundred years earlier, their Grandpa Sandy endured far greater challenges during his tour of duty than either my father or Uncle Van. Grandpa Sandy not only had to face possible death at the hands of his enemy, possible starvation, and widespread disease, but he also had to set himself and his brothers free from the cruel chains of slavery. I have no doubt that my father and Uncle Van would have been so honored to know that heroic Grandpa Sandy was part of our family.

Grandpa Sandy and his brothers must have been proud to be members of the USCT. It was a separate unit within the Union Army, consisting only of black soldiers initially led by white officers. In all, about two hundred thousand brave men served in the USCT. Throughout the South, black soldiers in battle clearly showed that they were brave and could fight well. In late 1864, Northern General George Thomas declared, "Gentlemen, the question is settled, the negro will fight."[10]

I'm sure that Grandpa Sandy and his proud brothers were great soldiers in the USCT and performed all tasks as required. They likely never fought in major battles, but that fact doesn't take away at all from their bravery. Every day, their lives were at stake, and, at any point, they could have been slaughtered by their fierce Confederate enemies.

War was difficult, and conditions were horrible for soldiers from both the North and the South. In 1863, a twenty-three-year-old nurse wrote of the horrors of war in a letter home to her family:

> A sickening, overpowering, awful stench announced the presence of the unburied dead upon which the July sun was mercilessly shining and at every step the air grew heavier and fouler until it seemed to possess a palpable horrible density that could be seen and felt and cut with a knife.[11]

Although the USCT soldiers were unfairly separated from the rest of the Union Army, I'm very grateful that Grandpa Sandy and his brothers were on the right side of the war—especially as the war shifted in the Union's favor by 1865. By now, the war that would claim more than six hundred thousand lives, both black and white, enslaved and free, was nearing its end.

As Grandpa Sandy and his fellow soldiers continued with their duties, they probably rejoiced when word spread that Confederate General Robert E. Lee had reluctantly surrendered to Union General Ulysses S. Grant on April 9, 1865. Finally, the Civil War was over. Grandpa Sandy was free at last!

Freedom, though, surely had its price. Less than one week after General Lee's surrender, on April 14, 1865, President Lincoln was shot by John Wilkes Booth. Lincoln died the next day. For Grandpa Sandy and other blacks, Lincoln's death was personal. Lincoln put his life on the line…and lost it. Although Lincoln entered the war in 1861 believing that his mission was to save the Union rather than to free the slaves, he accepted that the abolition of slavery was necessary to preserve the Union. The death of "Uncle Abe" Lincoln was a heavy blow for Grandpa Sandy.

As blacks lionized Lincoln's memory and legacy, they also quietly celebrated their newfound status. Yes, Grandpa Sandy Wills was finally a free man! He was about twenty-six years old when the war ended and had lived with the threat of death by war for about two years from 1863 to 1865. Like most other former slaves, Grandpa Sandy was probably cautiously optimistic when he learned that the Confederate troops had surrendered. After all, he had lived his entire life as a slave—an experience that had robbed him of his identity, his parents, his family legacy, and his education. He knew no other way of life. Grandpa

Sandy and his brothers in bondage may have been illiterate, but they could now hold their heads high. Thanks to their bravery, slavery was to be no more.

As the war ended, Sandy, Mack, James, Dick, and Andy likely marched with their heads held high as white officers repeatedly documented the outstanding conduct of the colored soldiers. Union Colonel Steven Hicks, who had initially opposed the enlistment of black troops, probably spoke the most dramatic words. He wrote, "Permit me to remark that I have been one of those men who never had much confidence in colored men fighting, but those doubts are now all removed, for they fought as bravely as any troops."[12]

Their efforts and bravery must have been a source of great pride for the Wills brothers. Dick Wills Parker was appointed a noncommissioned officer on October 5, 1865. Parker's upgrade was most certainly a very personal victory for all of the Wills men. They all marveled at the new stripe on the shoulder of Dick's blue uniform, a promotion that was well-earned and well-deserved. His stripe honored all the proud black men of the 4th U.S. Colored Heavy Artillery Regiment who championed the American flag even though the nation did not protect its children of color. But none of that mattered in 1865, because "nuth'in" tasted as sweet as their newfound freedom.

Grandpa Sandy was one of the lucky slaves who had the opportunity to fight directly against slavery. Unable to sign his name, he nevertheless brandished a weapon that was stronger than any gun—his sheer force of will. On February 25, 1866, the 4th U.S.

Colored Heavy Artillery Regiment was mustered out of service. Following the end of the war, celebrations of freedom were sweet but short-lived as millions of African Americans soon found themselves homeless and jobless. Their lives were in shambles. Many were desperate to reunite with children, parents, and other relatives who had been sold and separated from them during the bitter years when slavery reigned supreme in the South. Others wanted to get legally married and quickly assimilate themselves into society and begin to build new lives.

In 1865, the U. S. Congress established the Bureau of Refugees, Freedmen, and Abandoned Lands, also known as the Freedmen's Bureau, which addressed these needs of newly freed slaves. For a short while, the Bureau was effective in helping former slaves reconstruct their lives. It opened more than one thousand schools for blacks, along with a number of colleges. It's likely that Grandpa Sandy did not take advantage of these schools, but at least two of the Wills men did. Dick Parker and Mack Wills indeed went to school and learned to read and write! They no longer signed their names with a simple *X*.

Sadly, with every small step forward that the newly freed slaves took, many former Confederate soldiers and slave masters violently pushed them back. In 1865, Union General William T. Sherman mandated that African Americans take over the abandoned plantations in the South—forty acres per family—to resettle and rebuild their lives. In some cases, the army included a free mule to help newly freed slaves plow their plots. Within months, thousands of freed slaves took over these lands. But before the year was out, President Lincoln's successor, Andrew Johnson, revoked the order and returned the land to the former white owners. Some blacks worked out an agreement to remain on the property as sharecroppers, but others left in anger. President Johnson's quick decision to prevent former slaves from having their own land was a warning of what lay ahead for African Americans.

Even though the Fourteenth Amendment was ratified in 1868, stating, "All persons born or naturalized in the United States...are citizens of the United States and of the state wherein they reside,"[13] the days and years ahead would be filled with grave challenges for the newly freed slaves. Grandpa Sandy, Mack, James, Dick, and Andy all returned to Haywood County at the end of the war. Like many other penniless blacks whose primary skills were farming, Grandpa Sandy became a sharecropper. Given a small piece of land to farm, he was supposed to get a share of the profits from the crops he grew. But history shows that the illiterate sharecroppers were regularly cheated out of their fair share of the profits. Once again, they were in a "lose-lose" situation. The only difference was that now they could leave at any time they pleased. However, Grandpa Sandy didn't leave Haywood County, as it was the one place that he knew best.

Sometime around 1868, sweet Grandpa Sandy met a young woman at church who deeply touched his heart. Her name was Emma West Moore. The two were smitten. Born sometime around 1851, Emma was probably the picture of beauty at the age of sixteen when she met Grandpa Sandy. One census record describes her as being mulatto. The two of them lived about two-and-a-half miles from each other in Haywood County. According to Emma, they had never met before, although she reported that she had "known of his people,"[14] meaning his relatives or close friends.

On February 11, 1869, Sandy Willis Wills married Emma West Moore in what must have been quite an elaborate wedding for the two former slaves. As noted by Grandma Emma years later, "I was about 17 or 18 years old when I married Sandy Wills. I married him by license and there is a record of our marriage at Brownsville, Tennessee."[15]

Years later, Grandma Emma was required to describe in great detail many facts about her life with Grandpa Sandy in sworn depositions she gave while trying to get a widow's war pension following his death. The depositions are in her spoken words, but because she was illiterate, they were transcribed by her lawyers. These documents became a crucial part of my research, enabling me to learn all about my family's past. Thank you, Grandma Emma!

Grandpa Sandy and Grandma Emma's courtship was momentous. In generations past, slaves were often paired together, sometimes against their wills, to have children for the benefit of their slave owners. This practice was a particularly disgraceful slap at marriage. However, Grandpa Sandy and Grandma Emma were charting new territory. They were the first of many newly freed African Americans to decide on their own terms exactly whom they would marry.

Clearly, our Grandma Emma had maintained a strong bond with the Moore family even though she was previously a slave for them. As she stated in her deposition, "We were married on the Moore place right in the white folk's house."[16] Grandma Emma was especially close to Joel Moore, her former slave master's son. Indeed, he and the rest of his family were present at Grandma Emma's marriage ceremony to Grandpa Sandy. This warm relationship between former slaves and former slaveholders is not one that is typically discussed, but it should be. It's natural, especially for African Americans, to assume that all black slaves hated their white masters.

Surprisingly, our family history with slavery is not completely laced with hatred. I'm saddened and disgusted that my family had to suffer through slavery, but Grandma Emma apparently came through it without a trace of resentment or anger in her heart. I am angrier about slavery today, 150 years later, than she was when she actually lived through it. Grandma Emma apparently fully forgave—perhaps she was forgiving to a fault—the very people who had rendered her illiterate and not free to make her own life choices. I will never know why she apparently showed no anger toward the Moore family. Grandma Emma was graceful, affable, and extraordinarily forgiving, and she had no apparent feelings of hatred.

Perhaps Grandma Emma never fully accepted that she was being held against her will. She likely saw the Moore family as her own family and thus maintained a cheerful attitude. After all, she wasn't taken from her parents and sold into slavery as a young child, as was her husband, Grandpa Sandy. She was very close with her parents, Dolphin and Millie, and with all of her siblings. They remained together as a family for all of their lives. So with her perhaps naïve eyes, Grandma Emma had no problem getting married to Grandpa Sandy in the Moore family's big house.

In the popular view of the post-Civil War South, the relationships between blacks and whites produced a world full of resentment and even violence. Those reactions were obviously not part of Grandma Emma's brave new world of freedom. In 1869, just a couple of years after the United States of America finally recognized Grandma Emma as a human being and a citizen, she was happy, free, and in love.

The marriage of Grandpa Sandy and Grandma Emma was evidently the talk of Haywood County. A colored Methodist minister named Sam Williams traveled from Memphis to marry the young couple. The wedding was apparently a fancy one. Black and white guests were served dinner, and waiters were on hand as well. Of course, guests included Grandpa Sandy's beloved brothers: Mack, James, Dick, and Andy. I'm guessing that at least one of them served as his best man—though it's not explicitly known for a fact that his best man was a former brother in bondage.

The wedding might have also been the first time that blacks and whites ever mingled together in celebration at the Moore family's home. On the surface, the event was joyous, celebrating both marriage and emancipation for the first generation of African Americans in the South to be free from slavery.

After their splendid wedding day, Grandpa Sandy and Grandma Emma settled into a simple sharecropper house, which they did not own, and forged ahead. Grandma Emma continued to work as a beloved housekeeper at the plantation owned by the Moores, called Mooreland. Her new husband, Grandpa Sandy, a proud soldier who had ably mastered the techniques of warfare, was reduced, yet again, to picking cotton. For him, the sounds of gunshots in battle were but a memory and became a more distant echo with time. The proud, uniformed soldier had come full circle. He once again wore raggedy overalls and was working long hours in the cotton fields. Grandpa Sandy did his crucial part to end slavery, but, in some ways, nothing had really changed. Yes, he was free to walk away from Haywood County at any time, but where exactly would he go? He and Grandma Emma could have relocated to another town, but then they would have been isolated from their friends and family.

Following the end of the war, tensions were brewing in the South as different hate groups such as the Ku Klux Klan began to surface. The Klan was mostly made up of white, former Confederate soldiers who were determined to undo the successes that blacks had achieved in the wake of slavery. Klan members believed that white people were far superior to black people. Klansmen used violence and harassment to intimidate blacks—and the white people who helped them—in an effort to take away their basic civil rights. Through violence and organized political efforts, the Klan tried to prevent blacks from running for government office, building new businesses, and living peacefully in their own communities. The Klan's clear goal was to have white people live separately from black people, to terrorize them, and to force them to attend their own schools and churches.

As the bloody 1860s drew to a close, many white people had issued a virtual national memo stating that black citizens were to be shunned, shamed, and harassed. With the dawn of a new decade, white racists managed to convince millions of Americans that my great-great-great grandparents—and those who looked like them—were the scourges of society. This war was new, a battle of decency versus cruelty.

CHAPTER SEVEN

Emma's X

Does liberty entitle one to literacy?
Not as far as this eye can see.
Former slaves knew a single letter of the alphabet.
The dreaded "X" was the signature
which they boldly set.
They were never taught grammar,
vowels, or simple math,
But they hoped that their children
would forge a new path.
This is why I proudly sign my name,
With bold cursive strokes—for which
I have no shame.

As the South struggled to redefine itself during the early 1870s, Grandpa Sandy and Grandma Emma began building a new family. Their first child, a little boy, William Wills, was born on February 3, 1870, in Haywood County. Unlike his parents, who had been born into slavery, William entered the world as a free American citizen. The little boy would never be sold away under any circumstances. He would not ever be beaten or whipped if he wanted to learn how to read and write. His life belonged to his parents, not to a greedy slavemaster who would treat him like a mule. Grandma Emma and Grandpa Sandy had the privilege and the honor of loving their baby boy and teaching him how to survive in a free but still uncertain nation.

Grandma Emma and Grandpa Sandy blazed paths under the hot southern sun that would impact their family for generations. Grandma Emma recorded the day William entered the world, a first in her family. Although she was barely twenty years of age, she had developed a deep respect for recordkeeping. Grandma Emma was illiterate, but she realized that she had the historic opportunity to document her firstborn's birth, which is exactly what she did. That she couldn't write it down herself didn't matter. This data would be the first time that any records were ever kept to document her family. The Wills family would clearly no longer be ghosts.

Remarkably, Grandma Emma looked to the Moore family—her former slave owners—to help her record her new history. Master Moore's younger son, Joel, carefully wrote the name, birthday, and location of William's birth in a Bible that belonged to Grandma Emma. Over the next eighteen years, Grandma Emma would rely heavily on Joel Moore to record each of her children's births in her Bible. Referring to Joel Moore, she said, "He also set the dates of their birth down in my Bible as each one was born. I had nine children by Sandy Wills, eight of whom were living when [Sandy] died, and one was born the next month after he died."[17]

Joel Moore carefully wrote the details of each birth in Grandma Emma's Bible: Alex Wills, my great-great grandfather, was born on September 20, 1871. Sandy Wills, named for his courageous father, celebrated his birthday on August 8, 1873. Nicknamed Dolphin after Grandma Emma's father, Adolfus Wills was born on October 7, 1875. Grandma Emma's first girl, Mattie Belle Wills, was born on September 7, 1877, and John Henry Wills arrived on August 3, 1879. Walter Wills entered the world on January 25, 1883. A second girl, Priscilla, nicknamed Puss, was born on August 25, 1886, and the youngest, James, joined the family on March 28, 1889.

Apparently, few former slaves kept accurate records of their children's births. These new mothers were not negligent, but life must have been very dizzying for the former slave women. They now had to learn how to be traditional wives and mothers even though they couldn't read or write at all. When I reviewed the records of some of the other soldiers who fought with the USCT, their children's birthdays were usually not fully documented. I'm sure that the parents considered just recording the approximate year of birth to be an accomplishment.

Like Grandpa Sandy, Grandma Emma didn't need an education to know right from wrong. She had felt her way through the world, and her razor-sharp intuition guided her every move. Her signature may have been a humble *X*, but she saw to it that every single one of her children learned how to read and write! The 1900 census shows that Mattie Bell, William, John, and the youngest girl, Priscilla, who was thirteen at the time, were all documented as being able to read and write. That accomplishment is extraordinary for a young mother who was born a slave! Thanks to Grandma Emma's smarts, her Bible with the documented family names, and the U.S. Census, we know her many successes, now and forever.

Grandma Emma didn't fight in the Civil War like Grandpa Sandy did, but she was a soldier in her own right. She made sure that her children benefited from her husband's war-time sacrifice. A proud mother, she demanded for her children what she didn't have herself: a formal education. She set high standards for the entire Wills family for generations to come.

Grandma Emma had lived a life full of historic firsts. She also suffered from many painful blows. On February 8, 1889, Grandpa Sandy died. No record or explanation exists of how her brave soldier died. Sadly, Grandma Emma was pregnant with Little James when her beloved husband drew his last breath. According to Grandma Emma, "He [Grandpa Sandy] was 50 years old when he died."[18]

Grandpa Sandy fought for all of us. He was the handsome man whom Grandma Emma described as "dark brown, almost black in color, had black hair and black eyes and was…tallish…, but I can't give his exact height."[19] Grandpa Sandy left the world a proud man. A farmer, he died poor, but he kept his feet in the soil and his heart close to his family. He had a loving wife and eight children, with another one on the way. He and Grandma Emma did right by their children. The parents made sure that each child knew his or her exact date of birth, was able to read a book, and sign his or her name in full. All of the children would also be able to work and make money—no slave labor anymore. They all knew how to count their money, too.

Over the past few years, I have tried to find Grandpa Sandy's gravesite, but I do not know where he rests. The location of his grave is still a mystery to us. There is no record of his burial in any military cemeteries in Tennessee. I certainly hope to find his remains one day and honor him. Nevertheless, Grandpa Sandy will always remain forever buried in all our hearts. Shortly after Grandpa Sandy's death, Grandma Emma had to complete another courageous act. She applied for a widow's pension through the U.S. War Department. The process was long and painful, and she was treated like a lying criminal. The government made it much more difficult for black soldiers to receive pensions than it was for white soldiers. About 73 percent of white veterans were paid their pensions, while only about 48 percent of black veterans received their pensions. Grandma Emma was discriminated against every step of the way. Many of her personal documents have the word *Rejected* stamped in huge letters at the top of every page.

The problem for Grandma Emma was simple, although the solution would prove to be long and humiliating. The opening lines of Grandpa Sandy's discharge paper, officially filed on February 25, 1866, read as follows:

> Know ye, that Sandy Willis, a private of Captain Judson B. Francis Company G 4th regiment of the U.S. C. Art. Heavy, volunteers, who was enrolled on the thirteenth day of October one thousand eight hundred and sixty three to serve three years or during the war, is hereby discharged from service of the United States.[20]

Well, the error is clear. Grandpa Sandy's name is misspelled on this document, written as "Sandy Willis," not as "Sandy Wills." Of course, if Grandpa Sandy had been able to read, he would have simply corrected the misspelling during his discharge interview. But when Grandma Emma initially filed for her pension benefits, her application was rejected. The confusion and uncertainty must have been especially humiliating to her, a kind woman who could neither read nor write and who did not know how to work with lawyers and government officials.

In fact, Grandpa Sandy had filed an "Oath of Identity" form with the U.S. War Department Record and Pension Division in 1884 confirming that he personally appeared before a justice of the peace and that he was in fact the Sandy Willis in his discharge papers. He signed this document with his *X* signature. Nevertheless, the U.S. War Department ignored that documentation and coldly wrote to Grandma Emma: "The name Sandy has not been found."[21]

With that rejection in about 1890, Grandma Emma had to put into action a plan and a process to prove to the government and its literate lawyers that she was indeed eligible for her widow's pension. Her goal was to seek financial support for herself and her minor children, Mattie Bell, John, Walter, and Priscilla, all of whom were under the age of sixteen. The pension would provide each child with just $2 per month. In all, she hoped to receive $16 dollars per month, which is worth about $400 per month today. Brave Grandma Emma was surely preparing for a battle on all fronts.

Grandpa Sandy would have been proud of his warrior wife. She was steadfast and cautious as she figured out how to receive her pension. Throughout the battle to receive her pension funds, Grandma Emma was often humiliated by government officials. Many times, she wasn't certain about what she was being asked. The officials repeatedly asked her for the spelling of names and the birthdates of her children. She was bombarded with legal questions, too, but through it all, she always retained her gracious, gentle southern manners.

Grandma Emma put much of her trust in her lawyer, Mr. C.M. Sweet, who helped her navigate the process. He read all the necessary documents to her. Mr. Sweet also charged her ten dollars for his services, which was a large sum in the 1890s, especially for a poor, illiterate woman. Lawyers made a lot of money from black soldiers and their widows during this period. Not only did lawyers have to file each client's paperwork, but they also probably charged extra to do all the writing for those who were illiterate. Former slaves had no idea what was written on the government papers. Yet Grandma Emma worked hard and would not give up. She saw much and suffered plenty, but she never complained. Through it all, she remained poised and strong. Grandma Emma was our emancipated matriarch.

After three years, Grandma Emma got her first pension payment of sixteen dollars per month. And for about eight years thereafter, she often had to renew her application. The Department of Interior and the Bureau of Pensions Special Examination Division sent out dozens of questionnaires in an attempt to confirm Sandy's military experience. Their question was basic: "Do you remember the soldier Sandy Wills, aka Willis, as a member of your company?" During her battle with the government, Grandma Emma was helped by friends and other people who cared about both her and Grandpa Sandy. Former black soldiers like Abraham Dearborn, wrote, "I remember Sandy Wills well."[22] Other soldiers, like James Wills and another former slave, Jack Dyson, gave testimonials such as this one:

> We were fellow soldiers with Sandy Wills in the late Civil War and were mustered out together.... Claimant [Grandma Emma] has no property and no income except from her daily labor. We have known claimant since her marriage to Sandy.[23]

In the same way, loyal Andy Wills confirmed that he and Grandpa Sandy were slaves together: "I belonged to the same man he did before the war, lived and slept with him."[24]

Mack Wills also filed an affidavit to vouch for Grandma Emma's claim. He was one of the few black soldiers, along with Corporal Dick Parker, who could actually sign his full name, as opposed to signing with a simple *X*. Lastly, Corporal Parker stated, "I have known him since we were small boys and we belonged to the same man, Willis Wills, before the war."[25] I was intrigued by the fact that neither Andy nor any of the other witnesses referred to themselves as slaves or to their former owners as masters. These brave soldiers had obviously moved on with their lives with tremendous pride and dignity.

Of all of the very different affidavits and testimonies, none is more compelling than Grandma Emma's multiple depositions fully describing how she met her husband and just about everything else that happened during their marriage until his death. As always, one of Grandma Emma's biggest supporters was Joel Moore. In 1900, he gave yet another sworn deposition vouching for Grandma Emma's character. He wrote that he had known Grandma Emma all of his life: "She belonged before the war to my father, and she has always lived right around this neighborhood."[26] Furthermore, he stated, "I think she has lived a straight, honorable life. I have heard no talk at all against her character."[27]

Joel Moore even confirmed that he was the one who recorded the births of Grandma Emma's children when he wrote, "I do know that the ages of said children as recorded by me in said Bible are correct for the several entries were made by me soon after the respective birth when the date was fresh in my mind."[28] Joel Moore and many others who knew Grandma Emma wanted to support her application for the pension. Grandma Emma had many admirers. People cared deeply about her—whether they once owned her or not.

Throughout her ordeal, dear Grandma Emma had tremendous dignity, self-respect, and vision. She instinctively knew her efforts would not be in vain. She obviously possessed a sharp mind and never took her freedom for granted. Although she spent her entire life working for the Moore family, first as a slave and later as a paid laborer, Emma West Moore Wills laid the foundation for all generations of the Wills family. At times, I can almost hear her saying, "Make sure you stay in the books and learn all you can while you can."

The year 1893 was a sad year for Grandma Emma. Her young son, Little James, passed away at just three years of age in February 1893. Less than one month later, Sandy Jr., who was nineteen years old, died on March 22. Possibly, the same disease claimed both of them. Grandma Emma must have been devastated. The loss of two children within weeks is almost more than any parent could possibly bear.

Grandma Emma suffered more blows in 1898 when her oldest daughter, Mattie Bell, a wife and mother herself, died on November 28, just months after getting married. As Grandma Emma noted, "She died right here in my house."[29] Mattie Bell had married a man named Bill Bond. The couple had one child named Nales. Mattie Bell was just twenty-one years old when she passed away.

Grandma Emma gave so much of herself to so many people. She likely never had any time to herself. She was a multitasker before that term even became popular more than a century later. She tended to her husband, all her children, and her home every day, performing endless chores, from cooking and sewing to cleaning and organizing, without indoor bathrooms, electricity, or heat. She also managed to be a working mom, still making the short walk over to the Moores' big house to fulfill all her work tasks effectively and proudly—always.

Grandma Emma was rich in many ways. She kept the pressure on her children to learn to read and write. Despite her illiteracy, she fearlessly fought for her husband's pension that she fairly deserved. I would do anything and pay any amount of money to get my hands on Grandma Emma's Bible. I want to see with my own eyes how she knew that her children's lives were not in vain and that they would never be forgotten, all nine of them. During her life, she spent the bulk of her time tending to everyone's needs—except her own. The happiest and most carefree day of her life was probably her wedding day, when she may have donned a white dress or gown and fallen into the arms of her loving husband, the proud former soldier who had helped win the war against slavery. That day was probably the last time Grandma focused exclusively on herself.

I'm sad to report that our Grandma Emma died on May 31, 1901. A large group probably gathered to say a final farewell because most of her surviving children—except Puss and Walter, who were minors—were married with children. My great-grandfather, Allen Wills, who was also born in Haywood County, was about four years old when Grandma Emma passed away. Emma Wills, my brilliant, exquisite great-great-great grandmother, left her so-called mark on our lives in more ways than with just an *X*. Many hearts were broken when Grandma Emma died.

About eighty years after dear Grandma Emma's death, my heart was certainly broken when my father died in 1980. But thanks to my discovery of Grandpa Sandy and Grandma Emma, my emotional wounds have healed. I am no longer scared and fearful—now I'm daring and adventurous! They have given me the strength and courage to be brave, to care for others. I honor Grandma Emma's *X* as I now know that her *X* inspires me to "be eXcellent! Be eXtraordinary!

Be eXceptional!" Today, I feel like a twenty-first century soldier—marching in my ancestors' honorable footsteps, admiring them and learning from them with every step I take.

If my dad were alive today, he, too, would be proud to say that he was the great-great grandson of Grandpa Sandy and Grandma Emma. With his U.S. Army paratrooper wings emblazoned on his chest, he would have been humbled to know that Grandpa Sandy paved the way for his own military career. Indeed, like Grandpa Sandy, he, too, fought for freedom in his own special way, though his days were few. After all, Grandpa Sandy and Grandma Emma were the first in our family to jump and land on their feet. They were the original freedom fighters in our family. Thanks to them, we are all free today.

AFTERWORD

While conducting my research on Grandpa Sandy and Grandma Emma, I also focused on the family that "owned" them in Haywood County, Tennessee, the Moore family. The head of the Moore family was John Bertie Moore, JBM, the wealthy owner of the plantation aptly named Mooreland. My great-great-great grandparents, Sandy and Emma Moore-Wills, lived at Mooreland after the Civil War and remained there until they died.

John Bertie Moore was married and had four children. He died just before the Civil War broke out in 1860. Archived records, including receipts of JBM's estate, indicate that Grandma Emma's loyal father, Dolphin, became the substitute head of the plantation even before slavery ended. JBM's wife, Judith, apparently knew very little about managing the plantation, and neither did JBM's privileged children.

My research of the business papers of Mooreland helped me further investigate the slave culture that my family was forced into. I now have priceless pictures of the plantation, including the slave house (see book cover) that still stands. I learned how the Moores bought shabby items for their slaves, including my family members, like poorly made blankets and cheap clothing made of a coarse material called osnaburg. I also researched how the Moores bought and sold human beings with impunity.

During my research, I discovered receipts of bills for home schooling and colleges for the white children, but nothing similar at all for the black children on the plantation. Once again, it became painfully clear that illiterate slaves could only sign their names with an *X*, including all of the members of my family.

In reviewing the receipts, including the Moore family's frequent purchases of fancy items like silk kerchiefs and parasols, I understood firsthand how the Moore family got rich off of my own family's slave labor. Meanwhile, when my hero Grandpa Sandy died, he was flat broke, despite a lifetime of backbreaking labor.

This raw data is the unfiltered and uncensored truth about crimes against humanity that the United States of America sanctioned for generations. My family paid a dear price for these crimes, and I can clearly see how this disease of racism seeped into my family tree all the way to my father, who was born in 1942 during the height of the era of Jim Crow segregation laws and who bore witness to hateful signs that read, "Colored Only" and "Whites Only." My father was affected by those times, and I can't help but wonder how his life might have turned out if he had been treated like a human being when he was a kid.

Although I thoroughly enjoy researching the antebellum era from 1789 to 1869, there's nothing I can do to change it. Here's what I do know. The Civil War was a seminal chapter in American history and redefined what it meant to be an American. During Reconstruction, the years after the Civil War from 1865 to 1877, many schools were opened specifically for newly freed black children. U.S. Census reports from 1880 show that Grandma Emma and Grandpa Sandy's children were the first in my family who were able to read and write. As a journalist and lover of words, that's quite a big deal to me! Then the Fifteenth Amendment gave men like my Grandpa Sandy the right to vote, albeit a short-lived opportunity. Later, during the Great Migration from 1910 to 1970, Grandpa Fred fled with his family from Haywood County to New York City seeking a better life. Soon, technology made America smarter, faster, and more modern. More than a century and a half after slavery ended, I had the great pleasure of voting for the first African American president. And here I am, in the digital age, using a high speed modem to cut and paste together my family's lost lineage. It's been quite a ride from the quiet cotton fields of Haywood County, Tennessee, to the high tech newsrooms of New York City! I wouldn't trade it for the world.

Researching Your Ancestors

- ☐ Talk to your family members or guardians. Parents, guardians, grandparents, aunts, uncles, and cousins are your starting points. Ask them what they know about your family tree. Even rumors can be useful. Organize your family's information in a useful way:
  - Person's name
  - Photographs
  - Place and date of birth and death
  - Where he or she lived
  - Jobs he or she held
  - Hobbies, special interests, awards, etc.
  - Major events in his or her life
- ☐ Use online resources to identify your ancestors.
- ☐ Collect family records, including marriage and death certificates, diplomas, photographs, letters, postcards, and personal items.
- ☐ Search and focus on one last name at a time. Pick the branch of your family that was the most stable and lived in the same place for a long period of time. I chose the Wills family because many of its members lived in Haywood County, Tennessee, for more than a century, and thus they were easy to trace with census records.
- ☐ Visit the community where your family lived. Research the local cemeteries and libraries for further information, as well as local newspapers and archives.
- ☐ Share your findings with other members of your family by email or a blog.

Grandpa Sandy's Path to Freedom

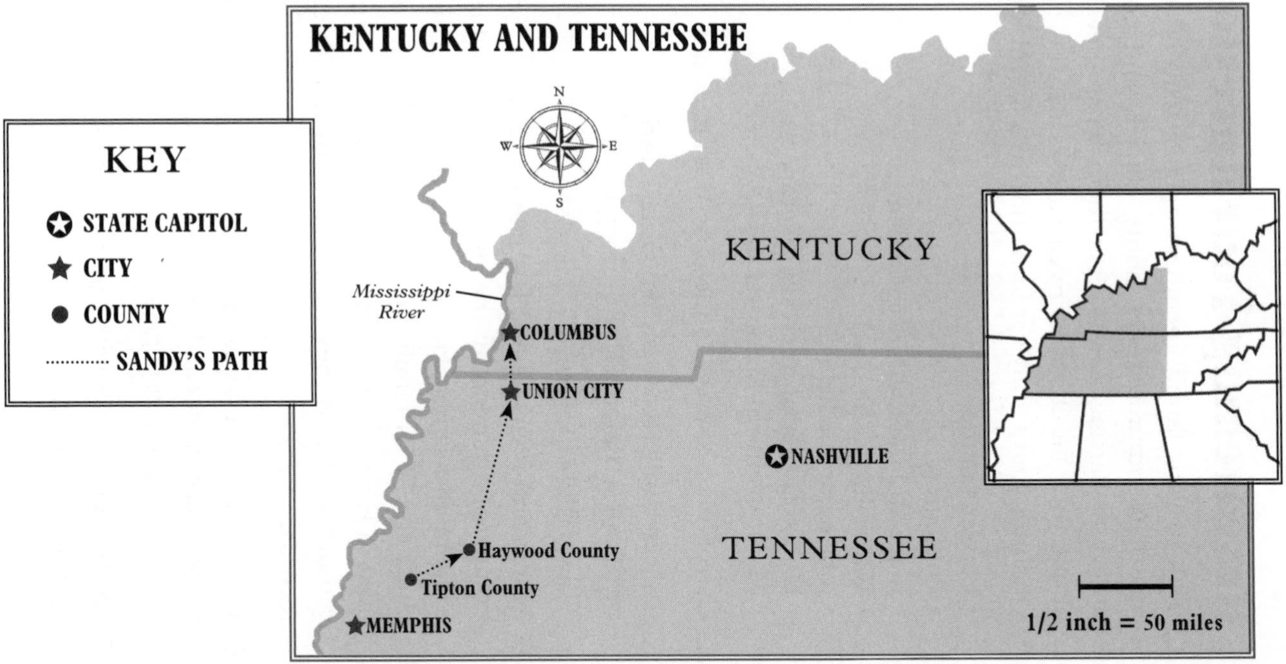

Depth of Knowledge

Discussion Questions

1. What questions would you ask the author in order to better understand the challenges she faced in writing about the perspectives and experiences of her ancestors?

2. The author describes various life lessons she learned from Grandpa Sandy, Grandma Emma, and her father. Select two life lessons written about in the book. What do they reveal about the author's purpose in writing this book?

3. What do Grandpa Sandy and Grandma Emma's signatures on the back cover of the book tell you about the impact of slavery on people's lives in the 1800s?

4. Discuss the different risks that slaves in the South took if they ran away to fight with the Union Army.

5. Determine the meaning of the following words as written by the author: "Jump, daughter, and figure out how to land later!" Analyze how the author uses these words throughout the book to help inspire readers.

6. The author's father frequently asked her, "What do you want to be when you grow up?" She often responded that she wanted to be a journalist. What types of jobs interest you? Discuss your choices.

7. President Abraham Lincoln declared in the Emancipation Proclamation "that all persons held as slaves [within the rebellious states] are, and henceforward shall be free." What conclusions can you draw about this historical period? Why do you think President Lincoln made this statement? Is this statement neutral or biased?

8. Look at the historical documents on pages 83-93. What evidence indicates that these documents are primary sources?

9. Is it important to learn about your ancestors?

10. Define freedom. Is freedom important to you?

Activities

1. The author introduces each of the chapters with a personal poem highlighting her perspectives about important themes in the book. Pick three of these poems. Write a paragraph for each poem to explain why it is meaningful to you.

2. Write an essay explaining how you overcame a difficult personal challenge in your life.

3. Write a speech to give to African American soldiers during the Civil War, thanking them for their bravery in fighting against the Confederacy.

Depth of Knowledge

4. Create a cartoon strip describing the emotions and challenges that Grandpa Sandy or Dick Wills likely experienced during their escapes from the Wills' plantation.

5. Develop a family tree. Interview older relatives and family friends for relevant information about your ancestors. (For more tips on creating a family tree, see page 123.)

Group Activity

History Comes Alive

Create a play about a well-known historical character that takes place both today and in the past.

1. Choose a historical character who appeals to the whole group.

2. Outline possible themes, points of view, additional characters, locations, and events in the play that are important to life long ago and today.

3. Structure the play into scenes—for example:

   Scene 1: Introduce principal characters, location, and themes.

   Scene 2: Identify the crises or problems that arise.

   Scene 3: Solve the problems.

4. Write the dialogue for each scene.

5. Rehearse each scene.

6. Perform the play in front of the class.

ENDNOTES: Primary Sources

1. Nick Chiles, "10 Disturbing Things About Slave Auctions in America You May Not Know," *Atlanta Black Star,* January 30, 2015, http://atlantablackstar.com/2015/01/30/10-disturbing-things-about-slave-auctions-in-america-you-may-not-know/.

2. Nick Chiles, *Atlanta Black Star,* January 30, 2015.

3. "What Was It Like to Be a Child Slave in the Nineteenth Century?" *National Archives,* Kew, England, http://www.nationalarchives.gov.uk/documents/education/childhood-slavery-contextual-essay.pdf.

4. "His Soul Goes Marching On, The Life and Legacy of John Brown," *West Virginia Archives and History,* http://www.wvculture.org/history/jbexhibit/jbchapter3.html.

5. "Black Troops in Union Blue," *Constitutional Rights Foundation,* http://www.crf-usa.org/black-history-month/black-troops-in-union-blue.

6. "I Would Save the Union," *Civil War Trust,* http://www.civilwar.org/education/history/emancipation-150/i-would-save-the-union.html.

7. "The Emancipation Proclamation," *The U.S. National Archives and Records Administration,* https://www.archives.gov/exhibits/featured-documents/emancipation-proclamation.

8. "The United States Colored Troops (USCT)," *Civil War Trust,* http://www.civilwar.org/education/history/usct/usct-united-states-colored.html.

9. "Dick Parker, United States Colored Troops"; Case Files of Approved Pension Applications of Veterans Who Served in the Army and Navy Mainly in the Civil War and the War with Spain ("Civil War and Later Survivors' Certificates"), 1861–1934. Records of the Department of Veterans Affairs, National Archives Administration (Washington, DC). Civil War and Later Pension Files, Records of the Department of Veterans Affairs, National Archives Administration (Washington, DC).

10. "The Color of Bravery: United States Colored Troops in the Civil War," *Civil War Trust,* 2013, http://www.civilwar.org/hallowed-ground-magazine/summer-2013/the-color-of-bravery.html.

11. Marissa Fessenden, "A Nurse Describes the Smell of War," *Smithsonian Magazine,* November 28, 2014, http://www.smithsonianmag.com/smart-news/nurse-describes-smell-civil-war-180953478/.

12. "African American Troops in Far West Kentucky during the Civil War: Recruitment and Service of the Fourth U.S. Heavy Artillery Colored," *The War of the Rebellion: A Compilation of the Official Records of the Union and Confederate Armies,* Series 1, Volume 32, part 1 (Washington, DC: Government Printing Office, 1880–1900), 548. Cited by William H. Mulligan in "African American Troops in Far West Kentucky in the Civil War: Recruitment and Service of the 4th U.S. Artillery (Colored)," p. 10, http://www.academia.edu/10152134/African_American_Troops_in_Far_West_Kentucky_during_the_Civil_War_Recruitment_and_Service_of_the_Fourth_U.S._Heavy_Artillery_Colored_.

13. "U.S. Constitution," *Legal Information Institute,* Cornell University Law School, https://www.law.cornell.edu/constitution/amendmentxiv.

14. "Sandy Wills and Emma Wills, United States Colored Troops"; Case Files of Approved Pension Applications of Veterans Who Served in the Army and Navy Mainly in the Civil War and the War with Spain ("Civil War and Later Survivors' Certificates"), 1861–1934; Records of the Department of Veterans Affairs, National Archives Administration (Washington, DC). Civil War and Later Pension Files, Records of the Department of Veterans Affairs, National Archives Administration (Washington, DC).

15. "Sandy Wills and Emma Wills, United States Colored Troops."

16. "Sandy Wills and Emma Wills, United States Colored Troops."

17. "Sandy Wills and Emma Wills, United States Colored Troops."

18. "Sandy Wills and Emma Wills, United States Colored Troops."

19. "Sandy Wills and Emma Wills, United States Colored Troops."

20. "Sandy Wills and Emma Wills, United States Colored Troops."

21. "Sandy Wills and Emma Wills, United States Colored Troops."

22. "Sandy Wills and Emma Wills, United States Colored Troops."

23. "James Wills, United States Colored Troops"; Case Files of Approved Pension Applications of Veterans Who Served in the Army and Navy Mainly in the Civil War and the War with Spain ("Civil War and Later Survivors' Certificates"), 1861–1934; Records of the Department of Veterans Affairs, National Archives Administration (Washington, DC). Civil War and Later Pension Files, Records of the Department of Veterans Affairs, National Archives Administration (Washington, DC).

24. "Andy Wills, United States Colored Troops"; Case Files of Approved Pension Applications of Veterans Who Served in the Army and Navy Mainly in the Civil War and the War with Spain ("Civil War and Later Survivors' Certificates"), 1861–1934; Records of the Department of Veterans Affairs, National Archives Administration (Washington, DC). Civil War and Later Pension Files, Records of the Department of Veterans Affairs, National Archives Administration (Washington, DC).

25. "Dick Parker, United States Colored Troops."

26. "Sandy Wills and Emma Wills, United States Colored Troops."

27. "Sandy Wills and Emma Wills, United States Colored Troops."

28. "Sandy Wills and Emma Wills, United States Colored Troops."

29. "Sandy Wills and Emma Wills, United States Colored Troops."

BIBLIOGRAPHY

"Abraham Lincoln." *Civil War Trust*. http://www.civilwar.org/education/history/biographies/abraham-lincoln.html.

"Abraham Lincoln and the Recruitment of Black Soldiers." *Journal of the Abraham Lincoln Association*. http://quod.lib.umich.edu/j/jala/2629860.0002.103/--abraham-lincoln-and-the-recruitment-of-black-.

"African American Records: Freedmen's Bureau." *The National Archives and Records Administration*. https://www.archives.gov/research/african-americans/freedmens-bureau.

Andrews, William, L., and William McFeeley, eds. *Frederick Douglass*. New York: W.W. Norton, 1996.

"Andy Wills, United States Colored Troops." Case Files of Approved Pension Applications of Veterans Who Served in the Army and Navy Mainly in the Civil War and the War with Spain ("Civil War and Later Survivors' Certificates"), 1861–1934; Records of the Department of Veterans Affairs; National Archives Administration (Washington, DC). Civil War and Later Pension Files, Records of the Department of Veterans Affairs, National Archives Administration (Washington, DC).*

"Bamileke." *Encyclopaedia Britannica*. 2009. https://www.britannica.com/topic/Bamileke.

Bateman, Robert. "Crime and Punishment in the Civil War." *Esquire,* November 14, 2013. http://www.esquire.com/news-politics/news/a25915/punishment-and-torture-in-the-civil-war-111413/.

"Battle and Surrender at Appomattox." *Civil War Trust*. http://www.civilwar.org/education/history/end-of-war/battle-and-surrender-appomattox.html.

"Black Soldiers in the Civil War." *The U.S. National Archives and Records Administration*. https://www.archives.gov/education/lessons/blacks-civil-war/.

"Black Soldiers in the Civil War: Preserving the Legacy of the United States Colored Troops." *The National Archives and Records Administration*. https://www.archives.gov/education/lessons/blacks-civil-war/article.html.

"Black Troops in Union Blue." *Constitutional Rights Foundation*. http://www.crf-usa.org/black-history-month/black-troops-in-union-blue.

"Cemeteries/Monuments." *Crossroads of War*. http://www.crossroadsofwar.org/see-the-sites/cemeteries-monuments/.

Chiles, Nick. "10 Disturbing Things About Slave Auctions in America You May Not Know." *Atlanta Black Star,* January 30, 2015. http://atlantablackstar.com/2015/01/30/10-disturbing-things-about-slave-auctions-in-america-you-may-not-know/.

The Civil War. Directed by Ken Burns. Florentine Films, 1990.

"Civil War Facts." *Civil War Trust.* http://www.civilwar.org/education/history/faq/?referrer=https://www.google.com/.

"Dick Parker, United States Colored Troops." Case Files of Approved Pension Applications of Veterans Who Served in the Army and Navy Mainly in the Civil War and the War with Spain ("Civil War and Later Survivors' Certificates"), 1861–1934; Records of the Department of Veterans Affairs, National Archives Administration (Washington, DC). Civil War and Later Pension Files, Records of the Department of Veterans Affairs, National Archives Administration (Washington, DC).*

Dobak, William A. *Freedom by the Sword: The U.S. Colored Troops 1862–1867 (American Civil War)*. New York: Skyhorse Publishing, 2013.

Douglass, Frederick. *My Bondage and My Freedom.* New York: Penguin Putnam, 2003.

Eggleston, Michael A. *President Lincoln's Recruiter: General Lorenzo Thomas and the United States Colored Troops in the Civil War.* Jefferson, NC: McFarland & Company, Inc., 2013.

"1800s Censuses." *Ancestry.com.* http://search.ancestry.com/search/category.aspx?cat=205.

"The Emancipation Proclamation." *The U.S. National Archives and Records Administration.* https://www.archives.gov/exhibits/featured-documents/emancipation-proclamation.

Fessenden, Marissa. "A Nurse Describes the Smell of War." *Smithsonian Magazine,* November 28, 2014. http://www.smithsonianmag.com/smart-news/nurse-describes-smell-civil-war-180953478/.

"Forty Acres and a Mule." *Blackpast.org.* http://www.blackpast.org/aah/forty-acres-and-mule.

"14th Amendment." *Cornell University Law School, Legal Information Institute.* https://www.law.cornell.edu/constitution/amendmentxiv.

"Frederick Douglass." *Mr. Lincoln and Freedom.org.* http://www.mrlincolnandfreedom.org/library/mr-lincolns-contemporaries/frederick-douglass/.

"Frederick Douglass American Abolitionist." *AmericanCivilWar.com.* http://www.americancivilwar.com/colored/frederick_douglass.html.

"Freedmen's Bureau." *Britannica.com.* 2015. https://www.britannica.com/topic/Freedmens-Bureau.

Gates Jr., Henry Louis. "Why Was Cotton King?" *WNET.* http://www.pbs.org/wnet/africanamericans-many-rivers-to-cross/history/why-was-cotton-king/.

"General Sherman Enacts 'Forty Acres and a Mule.'" *African American Registry.* http://www.aaregistry.org/historic_events/view/general-sherman-enacts-forty-acres-and-mule.

Glory. Directed by Edward Zwik. TriStar Pictures, 1989.

Goodstein, Anita S. "Slavery." *The Tennessee Encyclopedia of History and Culture.* http://tennesseeencyclopedia.net/entry.php?rec=1211.

Haley, Alex. *Roots.* Boston: Da Capo Press, 2014.

"A History of Slavery in the United States." *National Geographic Society.* http://nationalgeographic.org/interactive/slavery-united-states/.

Holzer, Harold. *A Just and Generous Nation: Abraham Lincoln and the Fight for American Opportunity.* New York: Basic Books, 2015.

"I Would Save the Union." *Civil War Trust.* http://www.civilwar.org/education/history/emancipation-150/i-would-save-the-union.html.

"James Wills, United States Colored Troops." Case Files of Approved Pension Applications of Veterans Who Served in the Army and Navy Mainly in the Civil War and the War with Spain ("Civil War and Later Survivors' Certificates"), 1861–1934; Records of the Department of Veterans Affairs, National Archives Administration (Washington, DC). Civil War and Later Pension Files, Records of the Department of Veterans Affairs, National Archives Administration (Washington, DC).*

"Ku Klux Klan." *History Channel.* http://www.history.com/topics/ku-klux-klan.

"Ku Klux Klan." *Southern Poverty Law Center.* https://www.splcenter.org/fighting-hate/extremist-files/ideology/ku-klux-klan.

"The Life of a Field Slave." *Fieldslaves.wordpress.com*, September 2012. https://fieldslaves.wordpress.com/2012/09/19/hello-world/.

"Mack Wills, United States Colored Troops." Case Files of Approved Pension Applications of Veterans Who Served in the Army and Navy Mainly in the Civil War and the War with Spain ("Civil War and Later Survivors' Certificates"), 1861–1934; Records of the Department of Veterans Affairs, National Archives Administration (Washington, DC). Civil War and Later Pension Files, Records of the Department of Veterans Affairs; National Archives Administration (Washington, DC).*

McClachlan, Sean. *The United States Colored Troops: The History and Legacy of the Black Soldiers Who Fought in the American Civil War.* Cambridge: Charles River Editors, 2016.

"Memorial and Museum History." *African American Civil War Memorial Museum.* https://www.afroamcivilwar.org/about-us/memorial-museum-history.html.

Mezurek, Kelly D. *For Their Own Cause: The 27th United States Colored Troops.* Kent, OH: The Kent University Press, 2016.

"Moore Family Papers, 1816-1819; 1824-1900." *The Tennessee State Library and Archives.* http://sos.tn.gov/tsla.

Mulligan, Jr., William H. *African American Troops in Far West Kentucky during the Civil War: Recruitment and Service of the Fourth U.S. Heavy Artillery (Colored).* https://www.academia.edu/10152134/African_American_Troops_in_Far_West_Kentucky_during_the_Civil_War_Recruitment_and_Service_of_the_Fourth_U.S._Heavy_Artillery_Colored_.

Olmstead, Frederick Law. *The Cotton Kingdom.* Boston: Da Capo Press, 1996.

"Population of Haywood County." *Population.us.* http://population.us/county/tn/haywood-county/.

"Richard Wills, United States Colored Troops." Case Files of Approved Pension Applications of Veterans Who Served in the Army and Navy Mainly in the Civil War and the War with Spain ("Civil War and Later Survivors' Certificates"), 1861–1934; Records of the Department of Veterans Affairs, National Archives Administration (Washington, DC). Civil War and Later Pension Files, Records of the Department of Veterans Affairs, National Archives Administration (Washington, DC).*

Rosenberg, John S. "Democrats Need a History Lesson on the Emancipation Proclamation." *National Review,* January 30, 2014. http://www.nationalreview.com/corner/369943/democrats-need-history-lesson-emancipation-proclamation-john-s-rosenberg.

"Sandy Wills and Emma Wills, United States Colored Troops." Case Files of Approved Pension Applications of Veterans Who Served in the Army and Navy Mainly in the Civil War and the War with Spain ("Civil War and Later Survivors' Certificates"), 1861–1934; Records of the Department of Veterans Affairs, National Archives Administration (Washington, DC). Civil War and Later Pension Files, Records of the Department of Veterans Affairs, National Archives Administration (Washington, DC).*

"Slavery in America." *History.com.* http://www.history.com/topics/black-history/slavery.

Smith, John David. *Black Soldiers in Blue: African American Troops in the Civil War Era.* Chapel Hill, NC: University of North Carolina Press, 2002.

Taylor, Susie King. *Reminiscences of My Life in Camp: With The 33D United States Colored Troops Late S.C. Volunteers.* Charleston: Nabu Press, 2014.

"10 Facts about the Emancipation Proclamation." *Civil War Trust.* http://www.civilwar.org/education/history/emancipation-150/10-facts.html.

"13th Amendment to the U.S. Constitution: Abolition of Slavery (1865)." *Ourdocs.gov.* https://www.ourdocuments.gov/doc.php?flash=true&doc=40.

"Union War Trophy: Fort Halleck." *Kygrro Post Details.* http://www.kygrro.org/columbusbelmontstatepark/.

United States Census Bureau. https://www.census.gov/.

"United States Colored Troops." *Civil War Trust.* http://www.civilwar.org/education/history/usct/usct-united-states-colored.html.

"United States Colored Troops Artillery." *Civil War Archive.* http://www.civilwararchive.com/Unreghst/uscolarty.htm.

"U.S. Colored Troops Military Service Records, 1863-1865." *Ancestry.com.* http://search.ancestry.com/search/db.aspx?dbid=1107.

"USCT History." *African American Civil War Memorial Museum.* https://www.afroamcivilwar.org/about-us/usct-history.html.

"War Department General Order 143: Creation of the U.S. Colored Troops (1863)." *OurDocuments.gov.* https://www.ourdocuments.gov/doc.php?flash=true&doc=35.

"What Was it Like to be a Child Slave in America in the Nineteenth Century?" *The National Archives (United Kingdom).* http://www.nationalarchives.gov.uk/documents/education/childhood-slavery-contextual-essay.pdf.

Williamson, Samuel H. and Louis P. Cain. "Measuring Slavery in 2011 Dollars." *Measuring Worth.* https://www.measuringworth.com/slavery.php.

Wills, Cheryl. *Die Free.* Minneapolis: Bascomb Hill, 2010.

Wills, Cheryl. *The Emancipation of Grandpa Sandy Wills.* New York: Lightswitch Learning, 2016.

Wilson, Sven. "Prejudice and Policy Racial Discrimination in the Union Army Disability Pension System, 1865-1906." *US National Library of Medicine, National Institute of Health,* April, 2010. https://www.ncbi.nlm.nih.gov/pmc/articles/PMC2837429/.

Zinn, Howard. *A People's History of the United States.* New York: HarperCollins, 2003.

* These files can contain supporting documents such as narratives of events during military service, marriage certificates, birth records, death certificates, family letters, statements from witnesses, and affidavits. A veteran's pension file can include his rank, place of residence, age or date of birth, and time of service. A widow's application can also include her place of residence, her maiden name, the date and place of marriage, the date and place of her husband's death, and the names of children under sixteen. A child's or heir's file contains information about both the veteran and the widow as well as the child's place of residence, date of birth, and the date and place of the widow's death.

Acknowledgments

Big hugs and lots of love to my husband, **John**, an elementary school principal whose devotion will always be sealed in my heart. Smooches to my one and only son, **John III**, who is on the fast track to success as a college freshman and budding track star at High Point University. Thank you, **Mommy**, aka Ruthie, for always being a rock in my life. A special shout-out goes to my mother-in-law, **Mary**, and my siblings, **Clarence**, **Crystal, Celestial**, and **Cleavon,** for your love and support. And, of course, the sixth Wills, **Emanuel Robinson**–my right hand-man!

A special thanks to my only surviving grandmother, **Opal Wills**, and my late grandparents, **Rev. Fred Wills**, **Rev. Hardy Ford**, and **Sallie Ford**.

And many thanks to **Steve** and **Ron Sussman** from Lightswitch Learning, a division of Sussman Sales Company, for their unyielding support of my many projects concerning my family's legacy from Tennessee to New York City. Thank you for supporting this book as well as the picture book *The Emancipation of Grandpa Sandy Wills*.

A big hug to editor par excellence, **Adam Reingold**, for digging deeply into the marrow of my story and turning it into a powerful family saga of which my ancestors, especially my father, would be proud. Thanks also to Dr. Rose Reissman for her support.

A fist-bump goes to my cousin, **Ethan West**. We connected online and found that we are both linked to our beloved Emma and her brother Henry. Thank you for traveling back to Haywood County and unlocking some of the mysteries surrounding our ancestor's bondage.

I would also like to acknowledge all of the **educators** and **administrators** whom I've met over the years who have opened their schoolhouse doors and welcomed me with open arms: **Principal Luis Torres** at P.S. 55 in the South Bronx. Principal Torres was elated to see his students gel to my story, and it was an extra special treat to capture their reaction in a national broadcast on ABC News. I would also like to thank principals like **Lawrence Burroughs** of the Ethan Allen School in Brooklyn, New York, and her superintendent, **Joyce Stallings Harte**, who invited me to their district multiple times to share words of encouragement to thousands of students and their parents. Those are life experiences that I will never forget.

Finally, I would like to thank two beautiful students I met: **Blessing Lawal** from the Bronx, New York, and **Anissa Ruiz** from Queens, New York. I met them on two different occasions. They slipped me very personal notes after I delivered a talk at their schools. I keep their notes in my bedroom on display.

Blessing wrote: *"Hello Ms. Wills, You are my hero–thanks for joining me and my friends for lunch."*

Anissa wrote: *"Dear Ms. Wills, I love your writing and your work and mostly, YOU!! P.S. Friends Forever."*

Blessing and Anissa are why I run to schools to share this story of empowerment. All students are precious, and I want them to know through the common bonds of our ancestors—no matter what cultural background—we are all friends forever.

Each one, reach one.

One Love,

Cheryl

CHERYL WILLS

Cheryl Wills is an anchor and senior reporter for Spectrum News Network's New York 1 News. Cheryl is the only journalist in the nearly twenty-five year history of the television network to conduct a one-on-one interview with a sitting President: Nobel Laureate Ellen Johnson Sirleaf of Liberia. The first woman President of Africa told Cheryl Wills exclusively about her administration's controversial handling of the recent ebola epidemic. Cheryl also conducted a sit-down interview with UN Secretary General Ban Ki-moon.

The award-winning journalist is the author of *Die Free: A Heroic Family Tale*. The acclaimed biography is about her great-great-great grandfather Sandy Wills' extraordinary transformation from a Tennessee slave into a courageous Civil War soldier, who honorably served with the United States Colored Troops from 1863 to 1865. Her second book is an illustrated children's version of her biography called *The Emancipation of Grandpa Sandy Will*s.

Cheryl Wills has traveled extensively, covering breaking news events, including the terrorist attacks of September 11, during which she reported from Ground Zero. She has reported from the White House and conducted interviews with Maya Angelou, Harry Belafonte, and many other global leaders.

Cheryl has received awards from the New York Press Club and the Associated Press. She also received the Newswomen's Club of NY Front Page award. UN

Secretary General Ban Ki-moon personally presented the United Nations Foundation Prize to her in 2015 at the United Nations Correspondents Association gala.

She has received the YMCA National Black Achievers in Industry award, the Carl T. Rowan Leadership in Media award, and, in 2010, McDonald's acclaimed her as a broadcasting legend.

In 2015, McDonald's again honored her with the first ever Harold Dow Lifetime Achievement award in recognition of her extraordinary and unparalleled contributions to broadcast media.

Cheryl Wills was the first journalist invited to speak before the General Assembly of the United Nations in 2011. She addressed the impact of slavery on her family during the UN's International Remembrance of Victims of the Transatlantic Slave Trade sessions.

She enjoys teaching students about the contributions of the black soldiers who fought valiantly during the Civil War. Cheryl is the founder and commander of the New York State chapter of the Sons & Daughters of the United States Colored Troops, a national organization based in Washington, DC.

Cheryl Wills is a graduate of the Newhouse School of Public Communications at Syracuse University, with a major in broadcast journalism. She received an honorary doctorate from the New York College of Health Professions in May 2005.

She is a member of the New York Association of Black Journalists, the New York Press Club, the Inner Circle of City Hall Journalists, the Screen Actors Guild, The Links, and the Women's Forum.

Adam Reingold, Editor

Adam is the author and editor of many children's books. He is currently an educational technology consultant with a focus on online personalized learning platforms. Previously, Adam directed content curation and publisher partnerships for Newclassrooms.org, as well as for the New York City Department of Education's School of One. He was co-founder of *Civcity.com*, an online platform for fostering interactions with great historical characters. He headed McGraw-Hill Education's Pre-K–6 social studies national marketing team, where he was previously editor of grades K-6 social studies products. Adam was a producer for the *Charlie Rose* TV show, a contributing editor for Peru's leading news magazine, *Caretas*, and editor of the New York City community newspaper, *Our Town*.

Photo Credits

Front Cover: (Clockwise from top left) Unidentified African American Soldier in Union Uniform, 1863–1865. Photo courtesy of Library of Congress Prints and Photographs Division; Slave Quarters, Haywood County, Tennessee. Photo courtesy of Ethan West; Clarence Wills, U.S. Army. Photo courtesy of the Wills Family Archives; Williamsburg Bridge, New York, New York. Photo Courtesy of Library of Congress Prints and Photographs Division.

Back Cover: (top left) Sandy Wills, Signature on Marriage Certificate. Photo courtesy of the Department of Veterans Affairs; (bottom left) Emma Wills, Signature on Deposition. Photo courtesy of the Department of Veterans Affairs; (top right) Clarence Wills, signature. Photo courtesy of the Wills Family Archives; (bottom right) Cheryl Wills' signature. Photo courtesy of the Wills Family Archives.

Title Page: See photo credits for front cover.

Page x: Emma Wills, deposition. Photo courtesy of the Department of Veterans Affairs.

Page xi: (top right) Clarence Wills, Fireman. Photo courtesy of the Wills Family Archives; (background photo) Cotton Field. Photo courtesy of Ethan West; Clarence Wills and Ruth Wills, wedding. Photo courtesy of the Wills Family Archives.

Page 45: Clarence Wills, fireman. Photo courtesy of the Wills Family Archives.

Page 46: Fred Wills, Statue of Liberty. Photo courtesy of the Wills Family Archives.

Page 47: (top) Opal Wills, 1941. Photo courtesy of the Wills Family Archives; (bottom) Clarence Wills, young boy at car. Photo courtesy of the Wills Family Archives.

Page 48: (top) Van Wills, Fred Wills, and Clarence Wills. Photo courtesy of the Wills Family Archives; (bottom) Van Wills and Clarence Wills, with guitars. Photo courtesy of the Wills Family Archives.

Page 49: Clarence Wills, with friend Frankie. Photo courtesy of the Wills Family Archives.

Page 50: (top) Sallie and Hardy Ford. Photo courtesy of the Wills Family Archives; (bottom) Clarence Wills, U.S. Army. Photo courtesy of the Wills Family Archives.

Page 51: (top) Clarence Wills and Ruth Wills, wedding. Photo courtesy of the Wills Family Archives; (bottom) Cheryl Wills, infant. Photo courtesy of the Wills Family Archives.

Page 52: (top) Fred Wills, Candyman. Photo courtesy of the Wills Family Archives; (bottom) Cheryl Wills, Clarence Wills Jr., birthday celebration. Photo courtesy of the Wills Family Archives.

Page 53: (top) Wills Family, Cheryl Wills and Clarence Wills Jr. Photo courtesy of the Wills Family Archives; (bottom) Cheryl Wills, portrait with plaid jacket. Photo courtesy of the Wills Family Archives.

Page 54: (top) Clarence Wills, New York City Fire Department truck and firemen. Photo courtesy of the Wills Family Archives; (bottom) Ocean Village buildings, New York. Photo courtesy of the Wills Family Archives.

Page 55: (top) Clarence Wills with motorcycle, car in background. Photo courtesy of the Wills Family Archives; (bottom) Clarence Wills, sitting in front of building. Photo courtesy of the Wills Family Archives.

Page 56: (top) Funeral of Clarence Wills, members of New Comers club. Photo courtesy of the Wills Family Archives; (bottom) Clarence Wills, casket with pall bearers. Photo courtesy of the Wills Family Archives.

Page 57: (top) Ruth Wills, with family. Photo courtesy of the Wills Family Archives; (bottom) Clarence Wills, gravestone. Photo courtesy of the Wills Family Archives.

Page 83: (left) Sandy Wills, United States Colored Troops Enlistment Form. Photo courtesy of the Department of Veterans Affairs; (Right) Dick Parker, United States Colored Troops Enlistment Form. Photo courtesy of the Department of Veterans Affairs.

Page 84: (left) Sandy Wills, Oath of Identity. Photo courtesy of the Department of Veterans Affairs; (right) Sandy Wills and Emma Wills, Marriage Certificate. Photo courtesy of the Department of Veterans Affairs.

Page 86: Emma Wills, deposition. Photo courtesy of the Department of Veterans Affairs.

Page 87: (top) Cotton field. Photo courtesy of Ethan West. (bottom) Slave quarters, Haywood County, Tennessee. Photo courtesy of Ethan West.

Page 88: (top) Mooreland sign. Photo courtesy of Ethan West; (bottom) Portrait of John Bertie Moore. Photo courtesy of the Tennessee State Library and Archives.

Page 89: (top) Allen Wills. Photo courtesy of the Wills Family Archives; (bottom) Collapsed church, Haywood County, Tennessee. Photo courtesy of Ethan West.

Page 90: (top) Cheryl Wills and Fred Wills, wedding. Photo courtesy of the Wills Family Archives; (bottom) Opal Wills and Fred Wills, anniversary party. Photo courtesy of Wills Family Archives.

Page 91: (top) Ruth Wills and adult children. Photo courtesy of the Wills Family Archives; (bottom) Cheryl Wills and Clarence Wills Jr., Apollo Theater. Photo courtesy of Wills Family Archives.

Page 92: President Barack Obama Certificate of Honor for Sandy Wills. Photo courtesy of Wills Family Archives.

Page 93: Wall of Honor, African American Civil War Memorial and Museum. Photo courtesy of Alonzo Boldin.

Page 139: Cheryl Wills. Photo courtesy of Alonzo Boldin.

Page 141: Adam Reingold, Photo courtesy of Jennifer Mirsky.

Illustration Credits

Page 85: (top) Young Sandy Wills at slave auction. Illustration by Randell Pearson. Courtesy of Lightswitch Learning; (bottom) Sandy Wills and Emma Wills with baby. Illustration by Randell Pearson. Courtesy of Lightswitch Learning.